HUNTING THE DIVINE FOX

HUNTING THE DIVINE FOX

Images and Mystery in Christian Faith

ROBERT FARRAR CAPON

A Crossroad Book
THE SEABURY PRESS · NEW YORK

The Seabury Press
815 Second Avenue
New York, N.Y. 10017

Copyright © 1974 by Robert Farrar Capon
Designed by Nancy Dale Muldoon
Printed in the United States of America

Library of Congress Cataloging in Publication Data

Capon, Robert Farrar.
  Hunting the divine fox.

  "A Crossroad book."
  1. Theology, Doctrinal—Popular works. I. Title.
BT77.C227   230   73–17891
ISBN 0–8164–0252–3

Ad Jerusalem
Si oblitus fuero tui . . .

CONTENTS

1
FABLE

ONCE UPON A TIME, IN THE MUD AT THE BOT-
tom of a tidal pool, there lived an oyster. By oysters' standards, he had a good life: The sea water was clean and full
of plankton, and the green warmth of the light at low tide
made him grow and prosper.

Next to him lived a stone with whom he sometimes
talked. It was very much the same size, shape and color as
he, and was good, if undemanding, company. As a matter
of fact, their conversations gave the oyster a definite feeling
of superiority. He loved to dwell at length on the differences that underlay their apparent similarity. Rocks, he
would say, are merely mineral. Oysters may be mineral on
the outside; but inside, they are bona fide members of the
animal kingdom.

One day, however, the stone surprised him by coming up
with a rejoinder. It pointed out that there were nevertheless
some advantages to being further down the evolutionary
scale. Rocks had fewer enemies than oysters. Starfish and
oyster drills, it observed, were no threat to stones; to the
oyster they were a matter of life or death. Furthermore,
the stone told him, it was getting just a little tired of being
put down by an oyster with airs. He might get a lesson in
humility if he would listen to some of the things starfish say

about oysters—things which the oyster never heard because he was too busy being mortally afraid, but which the stone heard regularly, and with amusement.

Starfish, it seems, have a very low opinion of oysters. They eat them, but they always refer to them as "nothing more than a rock with a stomach." In fact, what passes for humor among starfish is rather like Polish jokes, except that the punch line invariably has to do with how stupid it is to be an animal and not be able to move about. The worst thing one starfish can call another is "sessile creature."

The oyster terminated the discussion huffily and went into a state of profound depression. To have everything he had been so proud of become the butt of underwater ethnic wisecracks made life not worth living. Existence, he concluded, was nothing but a cruel joke. All the faith he once had in the grand design of the evolutionary scheme forsook him. Better to believe in nothing than dignify this farce of a world with pretensions of order. He became an anti-evolutionist, and stopped saying his prayers.

For a while, righteous indignation made the losing of his religion rather fun, as it always does; but as summer wore on into fall and the water began its slow progress to winter's cold, he became merely sour—angry at the universe, but even more angry with himself for having let it turn him into a grouch. Finally, in desperation, he decided he would pray once again; but this time with a difference. No more mumbling of set pieties. He saw himself as a Job among oysters; he would open his shell and curse his day.

And the oyster spoke and said, "Let the day perish wherein I was spawned, and the night in which it was said, A seed oyster has appeared. Why is light given to him that is in misery, and life to the bitter in soul? Why do I live my days in doubt and darkness? O, that one would hear me, and tell me openly of the glories above. Behold, my desire is, that the Almighty would answer me."

And, to his utter astonishment, a voice said, "All right, all right. But I have to make it short. It's Friday afternoon.

"It's all true. There are things you never even dreamed of. All kinds of stuff. And with moves you couldn't imagine if you tried. As a matter of fact, that's your problem. There you sit with a rock on one side and a starfish on the other. My apologies. It's a limited field of vision, I admit, but in the evolutionary-scale business, you've got to put a lot of things near the bottom. Spoils the effect if you don't.

"Anyway, the moves. I'll tell you a few. Basketball. College basketball, especially. The best ones are so flashy, they make you laugh for not being able to believe the guy actually made the shot. And squirrels going through trees. One of my best effects. You know the last time a squirrel missed his footing? I keep track of these things. It was May 3rd, 1438. Definitely a record.

"And it's not all slapdash, either. I've got creatures so graceful, they almost break your heart. When it comes to exquisite moves, my favorite maybe is girls' knees. Lovely. Some people think that's a funny thing to get excited about, but in this line of work, there's no substitute for enthusiasm.

"Seriously. If you take the knee thing and really go all the way with it, you get my absolute favorite for loveliness, a prima ballerina. Talk about moves. It's like Ernie DiGregorio, Marcel Marceau and Squirrel Nutkin all rolled together—but as a girl, which makes it that much better. Terrific.

"Listen, though. It's almost sundown, and I have to set a good example. As I said, your basic problem is your point of view. There really are all these great moves, but you unfortunately don't know from motion. If you're going into business as the world's first philosophical oyster, it's O.K. by me. But just so you shouldn't get it all wrong, I'll give you one piece of advice: Think very carefully. Remember that all this stuff really is, but it can't possibly *be* the way you *think*. Or, to turn it around: The way you *think* about things will never be exactly the same as the way they *are*. But enough. I really have to run. *Mazel tov*."

And with that, the voice ceased and the oyster was left alone with his thoughts. He felt both humbler and more elated than ever before. He resolved to philosophize no matter what the difficulties, and, in order to make the best use of the voice's advice, he decided to put himself in a methodical frame of mind. What follows is a transcript of his train of thought.

1. There is motion. I, as an oyster, can distinguish two sorts. The first is *being moved* (e.g., both the stone and myself can be moved by oystermen). The second is *moving* on one's own. The stone cannot do this at all. I can move the part of myself within my shell but I cannot move my whole self from place to place. The starfish can move from place to place.

2. The voice was quite clear on the existence of more mobile creatures than the starfish. Let me see what I can say about the prima ballerina:

> *Starfish move; ballerinas move.*
> *Starfish attack oysters.*
> *Can starfish attack ballerinas?*

This is problematical. Perhaps a tentative solution would

be that since the ballerina's motion is apparently far more eminent than the starfish's, a ballerina would invariably move in such a way as to avoid starfish. There are unresolved difficulties however:

    a. I do not know whether starfish and ballerinas occupy the same medium.

    b. I do not know whether starfish have any interest in attacking ballerinas.

3. Let me begin again:

> *Starfish move; ballerinas move.*
> *Starfish are deadly to oysters.*
> *Are ballerinas deadly to oysters?*

One line of approach would seem to be that, since the voice says that ballerinas are his absolute favorite for loveliness, and since loveliness and deadliness do not seem to be compatible, the ballerina cannot be deadly to the oyster. (This depends, of course, on what is meant by loveliness and deadliness. It also might depend on whether a ballerina's possible deadliness to the oyster proceeds out of her nature, as the starfish's does, or out of some accidental or acquired taste, as it were. If the latter were true, then it might be that not every ballerina is deadly to oysters.) In any case, there is not enough evidence to resolve the question.

4. Even though the voice's enthusiasm for the world of higher motion seems to have suspended my own doubts, it is disturbing to think how easily a skeptical oyster could argue from all this that ballerinas do not

exist, but rather are nothing more than a distracting hypothesis invented by oysters who cannot face the grimness of existence without flinching.

5. Tentatively, I shall list the following as the chief properties of the prima ballerina:
   a. Mobility (like the starfish's, but better).
   b. Invulnerability to starfish (likely).
   c. Loveliness (on faith).
   d. Deadliness (possible, but not certain).
There is a good deal unresolved here. Perhaps it would be useful to consider next what ballerinas are for. This is fascinating but tiring. At least, though, the sea water seems refreshing again.

CHINESE PROVERB
He who hammers at things over his head
easily hits nail right on thumb

2
ANALOGIES

—AND HE WHO HAMMERS HIGHER DOES IT
easier still.

Unless our philosophical oyster gets a firm grip on the
truth that discourse about realities other than himself is always couched in analogies, parables, images and paradoxes,
he could very well conclude his definitive treatise *On The
Prima Ballerina* by proving that ballerinas have five feet and
glide along the ocean bottom at four miles per hour. And
unless we, who are unfathomably further from our major
subject than the oyster, are a hundred times more careful,
we will say even stranger things about God—and be just as
unaware as the oyster that we have almost completely missed
the mark.

That is why the very first word in theology has to be not
about God, but about the way we ourselves use words.
Specifically, it has to be a firm warning that no words of ours
can ever be trusted to mean the same thing when predicated
of ourselves and God. Not even the florid ones with Greek
and Latin roots. True enough, God is merciful and God
is good, and you may make him out to be as omnipresent,
immutable and omniscient as you please. But never think
for a minute that you have anything more than the faintest
clue to what it's actually like for him to be all those things.

You may assume on faith that it is legitimate to use such words, but never forget the oyster and the ballerina: She can grasp his brand of motion better than he can hers. When you're on the low end of an analogy, be very slow to decide you know what the upper end is all about.

Once that warning is digested, however, the going gets a bit easier. Some people, for example, try to attack theology by claiming that human discourse about God is invalid because it is anthropomorphic. On examination, however, the apparently lethal paving block thus flung turns out to be a cream puff. Of course our language is anthropomorphic. We are men, and human words are all we have: Even the Word of God is composed totally of the words of men. But for all that, no theologian seriously suggests that God is just a big man. The nature of analogy, scrupulously kept in mind, is a constant reminder that we are ignorant of more than we know about God—that we know far better what he isn't than what he is.

"Ah, but," the objector says, "if analogy is the only way you have to talk about God, why talk at all? Stick to statements in which words can be used with one meaning only."

Well, on that basis, nobody will make very many statements about anything. One of the biggest pieces of mischief in our thinking is the assumption that talk about God is a special case, and that the rules which apply to it apply to nothing else. Admittedly, God himself is a special case; but our talk about him is just plain talk. The objection to the use of analogies when talking about God presumes that they are a strictly theological device of questionable validity. The fact is that we use analogies not only when we talk about what is over our heads, but all the time—whenever we talk about anything, up, down or sideways.

When I say my dog knows the way home from the other

side of town, I am making just as full a use of analogy as when I say the Lord knows all things eternally. True enough, there is not as much temptation to think of my dog as a little four-legged man as there is to think of God as a big invisible one, but the same rules apply.

Consider. My dog is doing something. He's getting from the other side of town to his doggie dish just in time for dinner. He was not dragged home with a rope, or mailed home in a box; he came home on his own. He alone, of course, is the only one who is really aware of the process by which he got there; but if I want to feature to myself how he did it, I am going to have to cast about for an analogue out of my own experience. Along with most of the human race, I don't take too long to find a good one: I say, he *knows* the way.

I would be foolish, of course, to think, having said that, that I have any direct, univocal understanding of how he knows. His ways are not my ways any more than God's are. But for all that, few sane men have much trouble with the device. And even those who go to insane lengths to avoid it invariably fall right back into it.

Suppose, for example, I decide to explain my dog's trip home for dinner, but to avoid the use of such anthropomorphisms as *knowing* I cast about for something else. Ah, I have it. Some force propelled him. How shall I speak of such a force? Perhaps I shall say that the omnipotent will of God kept him unswervingly in right paths. Or, if you would like something less pious, I could say that an unbreakable chain of causes, programed into the universe from day one, did the same job on him. But look what I have done. I have thrown out a really apt—and, above all, bare-faced—analogue like knowing, and substituted for it a couple of silly and sneaky ones. For after all, any will of God that a dog can't get away from is just a pious way of smuggling in the suggestion of the leash; and inescapable determinism is nothing more than Latin for a philosophical box to mail him home in.

Indeed, one of our troubles, not only in theology, but all the way down the line, stems from our failure to use the best, most human analogues we have. Take the case of the sunflower, for instance. We are so impressed by the scientific clank of subhuman comparisons that we feel we ought not to say that the sunflower turns because it knows where the sun is. It is almost second nature to us to prefer explanations that sound like the speech of a troll with a large vocabulary. We are much more comfortable when we are assured that the sunflower turns because it is heliotropic.

The trouble with that kind of talk is that it is nowhere near analogous enough. It tempts us to think we really know what the sunflower is up to. But we don't. The sunflower is a mystery, just as every single thing in the universe is. The world is a tissue of beings, each of which, like Eliot's cat, is the only one who knows its own deep and inscrutable singular Name. We do indeed know each other, but only by knowing the names we decide to call one another. And we can indeed know what other creatures are up to, but only by featuring to ourselves what it would be like if we were doing it. And it's all legitimate. And it works like a charm. But the delicious mystery of the self-identity of each creature still remains the mystery it always was.

One of the benefits of theology is that if you ever get anything right on the subject of God, you immediately get a bonus and start getting things right about the world. As soon as you realize that it is possible to talk about God in human terms and still utterly respect the mystery of his being, you quickly find that if you take the same care for creatures, the taste of the mystery of their being comes rushing back. It's like blowing your nose when you can't smell a thing and suddenly discovering that the glassful of nothing you were drinking is Cos-d'Estournel '45.

Let us have, therefore, not less anthropomorphism, but more. We must remember the oyster, of course, and avoid the mystery-stealing silliness of thinking that cats actually conceptualize as we do, or that stones literally make up their minds. But having done that, we are in a position to reclaim that older, better reading of creation which only the best analogies give. Think of what it would be like to have with us once more dogs who *know,* sunflowers who *like,* great stones which *refuse* to budge and rivers which *make glad* the City of God. Imagine getting back a universe moved by *love* for the good, full of creatures who are *priests* for each other, with heavens that *declare,* waters that *rage,* stars that *sing* and a sun who once again can *rejoice as a giant to run his course.*

It really was a better world—and our foolishness about words is the only reason we have to put up with the sleazy substitute we're making do with right now.

3
PROOFS

BEFORE GOING ON WITH THE WORK OF REC-
lamation, however, let me offer you a few apologies and
explanations.

Even this early in the conversation, you may have begun
to suspect in me a tendency to assume the truths of Christianity without proof. If so, you are right—except that it is
more a principle than a tendency. The important points
from which a dogmatic theologian works are seldom sus-
ceptible of proof—and the points which he can prove are
usually not very important. I realize, however, that this runs
contrary to what most people expect from a theologian. To
them, projects like Proving The Existence Of God sound
like the theologian's proper work, and they seem to expect
anyone who neglects such tasks to feel ashamed of himself.

As I said, I am constitutionally unrepentant on the subject; but I shall, nevertheless, offer you an apology of sorts
for this absence of apologia.

To begin with, it is seldom understood how modest the
results of any proof of the existence of God must necessarily
be. (Not that I agree with the apparent majority of philosophers and theologians who say it can't be proved at all, or
that, if it can, it can be demonstrated only as a probability,
and not as certainty. I am convinced it can be demonstrated

13

—and demonstrated beyond a doubt, if you use nice tight arguments like St. Thomas's "Five Ways.") The important point to make about the proofs is that even at their convincing best, they just wing God on the ear lobe, as it were. They don't tell you much.

Notice how they work. They take a look at the world and conclude that its nature is such that it absolutely requires, let us say, a first cause which is itself uncaused. So far so good. But then they take a turn which almost nobody bothers to notice. They do not say:

> *God is an uncaused first cause;*
> *An uncaused first cause exists;*
> *Therefore God exists.*

The major premise of that syllogism is an impossible statement. Nobody knows beans about what God is. The best we can say is this: One of the notes of the judaeo-christian concept of God is the notion that he is an uncaused first cause. What we have proved precisely, therefore, is that one of the notes of that concept actually exists. Notice what exceedingly minor stuff this is. You haven't reached God himself—you never do; you haven't really even nicked his ear lobe. The most you can claim is that you have established the existence of at least one thumbprint which a lot of people have included in their dossiers on him.

Why then the enthusiasm for proofs? Well, a lot of it was due to the fact that too many Christians never noticed how the proofs proceeded, and thought they proved a good deal more than they do. Aristotle was the first one in this philosophical tradition to think his way through to an uncaused first cause. As far as we know, however, he did not fall down on his knees and worship it. Rather, he just went on with his main point—which was, since he was a highly talented philosopher, to continue his virtuoso philosophizing.

St. Thomas, however, was another case. His main point was not philosophizing, but falling down on his knees to worship the God of the judaeo-christian revelation whom he knew as, among other things, the Three Persons of the Holy and Undivided Trinity, the God of Abraham, Isaac and Jacob, and the Uncaused First Cause of the world.

Now when Thomas, who also happened to be very good at philosophizing, came across Aristotle's proof of an uncaused first cause, he stopped dead in his tracks and said something that never could have occurred to Aristotle. He said, "Hey! I know who that is! That's my main point! Fancy being able to prove by reason the existence of something I held only by faith up till now." Reason does the proving, you see, but it's faith that's responsible for the enthusiasm.

That is why I give you only a half-hearted apology for not doing much proving. You will be interested in God's existence only if, in advance of proof, you care about the subject. And that depends on more than mere existence. What does it matter to you if I can prove that lobsters exist, if you don't like lobsters? The theologian's real job should be to work up your enthusiasm for the Lobster Himself. Only after that can he talk about the Unlobstered First Lobster without putting you to sleep.

Theologians, therefore, are to be judged more by the quality of the information they give than by the evidential force of the arguments they make. You should demand of them discussions of the really important things you have to know in order to make up your mind. Not, Does God exist? Rather, What is he like? Is he nasty or nice? Does he wear overpowering aftershave? Does he force Chinese food on his friends?

What you will get from me, accordingly, is precious little proof, but lots of excursions into the fearful and wonderful world of what the christian revelation has to say about God. Note, however, this does not mean that I am about to answer your questions. Any questions you—or I—could ask in advance of our examination of the faith would more than likely be just as oysterish as the ones I just suggested, even if they sounded much more sensible. What I am about to give you instead is a guided tour of selected spots in the bizarre set of answers that I believe God has given us. Then, perhaps, we may inch our way back to a point at which we will be able to ask better questions. I do it that way because I am convinced that accepting the revelation on faith is the really *interesting* enterprise.

Theologians of an earlier day, with just a little blowing of their own horn, called theology the Queen of the Sciences, because it dealt with the highest class of subject matter. Philosophy, they said, was great—the overarching science of all the sciences, even of theology—but it had, by definition, to deal only with what mere human beings could wring out of creation by force of reason. Theology, on the other hand, started from nothing less than the revelation of God himself. It began its trip on the road to knowledge well beyond the point at which philosophy ran out of gas.

Nowadays that has a quaint, old-fashioned ring to it; but something like it needs reviving. Perhaps the way to say it is that philosophy points the searchlight of intelligibility at God and comes up, at best, with a few sightings. Theology, on the other hand, doesn't hunt for God that way at all. Instead, it receives in the mail a gross of very odd flashlights from the Lux Invisibilis Flashlight Co. It then takes these and proceeds to point their mysterious light not only at God,

but also at creation and, in the process, discovers movements, shapes and colors it never saw before.

Theology, therefore, is fun. The inveterate temptation to
make something earnest out of it must be steadfastly re-
sisted. We were told quite plainly that unless we became as
little children, we could not enter the kingdom of heaven,
and nowhere more than in theology do we need to take the
message to heart. Accordingly, what we shall be up to here
is playing—even horsing—around with the flashlights just
to see what we can see. If you'd like a more sedate and respectable description of it, say we are acting in accordance
with Psalm 36, verse 9, which also happens to be the in-
scription over the chapel of Columbia University: "*In
lumine tuo videbimus lumen.*" Or say that, in the words of
the ancient Greek evening hymn, we are allowing the *phos
hilaron,* the "gladsome light," to shine in our minds. (Do a
little better than "gladsome" if you will, though. It sounds
so moderate and Victorian. Maybe *hilarious?*) But whatever
you do, keep it light, or it won't, obviously, be light at all.

One last apology. Among the many other things I shall not
be offering to prove, there is one which lies at the heart of
everything I have to say: It is the validity of our knowing
process. Many philosophers who weigh in at a lot more than
I do have exercised themselves on the subject—and so
strenuously that I long ago decided to take the whole thing
as a spectator sport. With TV tuned, therefore, and Barca-
lounger tilted back, my one comment on epistemology is
that I root for any team which says human knowledge is
valid, and never watch the others.

I do this because everybody I know acts as if it were valid
anyway. The skeptic is never for real. There he stands, cock-
tail in hand, left arm draped languorously on one end of

the mantelpiece, telling you that he can't be sure of anything, not even of his own existence. I'll give you my secret
method of demolishing universal skepticism in four words.
Whisper to him: "Your fly is open." If he thinks knowledge
is so all-fired impossible, why does he always look?

So no epistemology here. A little attention, perhaps, to
some of the light theology can shed on the way our minds
work, and a lot to what should probably be called theological
semantics, but which I prefer to think of as fooling around
with the intellectual images by which we pick up God, Man,
Christ and the Church. But definitely no epistemology. And
no more apologies either.

4
WORDS

IT WAS ON A FRIDAY AFTERNOON, BACK AT
the beginning of when, that God said the one thing which
probably has given him more trouble than anything else:
"Let us make man in our image, after our likeness: and let
them have dominion over the fish of the sea, and over the
fowl of the air, and over the cattle, and over all the earth,
and over every creeping thing that creepeth upon the earth."
And because God can't even think anything without having
it jump out of nothing into existence, the result was that
God created man in his own image, in the image of God
created he him; male and female created he them.

In the old days, when theologians were less uptight about
their respectability in the eyes of biblical critics, the odd,
majestic plural of that fateful "Let us make" was always
taken as one of the Old Testament evidences for the doctrine
of the Trinity. Nowadays you lose your union card if you
do things like that, but I still think it's nice. You don't have
to be dead earnest about it all and work up a theory that the
Jewish writer who put the first chapter of Genesis together
was some kind of crypto-Christian, or that the Holy Spirit
was deliberately trying to Tell Us Something. After all, the
Spirit got in his decisive innings on the Trinity later on, with
Jesus and Paul; and as far as Christians are concerned, the

19

LORD God who made the world just had to be the Holy Trinity anyway. What's nice about that "us" is precisely its oddness. It's the kind of mysteriously gratuitous detail which is so much fun to come across in the work of a master craftsman. "Hey!" you say, "look at that! Why would he say such a thing? He must smoke chicken marrow or something."

See? You need to *play* with Scripture, or else you get it all wrong. Deriving the doctrine of the Trinity from the "us" is nothing more than a little bit of baroque ornamentation: It's legitimate as long as you keep things in balance. The people who object to it do so because they think it's a case of putting a big doctrinal construction on top of a little grammatical point. But they're wrong. In theology you're in the oddity and style business. Once you get that straight, then the "us" is no longer a minor point; it's a mark of style. You may not know exactly why it's there, but you feel it's trying to tell you something, trying to elicit some kind of response from you. It just *asks* for ornamentation. So when the old boys put in a few trinitarian trills, they weren't destroying the balance of the piece; they were just making it sound—well, *nice*.

Let me give you another instance.

God says, "Let *us* make man. . . ." Nowhere else in the whole first chapter does he use this form. All the other creatures are sprung out of nothing with a rather impersonal "Let there be. . . ." From light to firmament, to land, to herb; from sun to stars, to whales, to fowls, to cattle, God is interested, but he doesn't seem involved. But when he gets to man, he really puts himself into it. He rolls up his sleeves, rubs his hands together and says, "Now comes the part *we* always love best!"

And that, Virginia, is why man is in the image of God.

You see? It's perfectly serious and perfectly silly at the same time. Which is just great. It's like making love: You can laugh while you do it. As a matter of fact, if you don't, at least sometimes, you're probably a terrible lover. Watch out for biblical commentators, therefore, who sound as if they're holding a sex manual in the other hand. And especially watch out for the kind who look down their long theological noses at St. Paul for proving that the Gospel is above the Law from the minor fact that "Abraham's *seed*" is in the singular and not the plural. Dummies! He was not trying to make an intellectual fast buck out of Scripture. He was making love to it.

But enough pique. Before I was derailed by my annoyance at biblical critics, I was working up to the subject of man in the image of the Trinity.

According to christian doctrine, creation arises out of a mysterious interaction within God himself—out of some kind of exchange between the Persons of the Trinity: Father, Son and Holy Spirit. The Son and the Spirit, therefore, are in the act from the beginning. They don't wait until the New Testament to go to work; all three Persons create, because they are, all three, simply the one and only eternal God there is. (It's confusing, I know, but don't think about it. It's a flashlight. We're not going to look at *it;* we're going to point it at the world. Focus the beam a little more narrowly, though.)

When we talk about the role of the Son in the act of creation, we normally refer to him as the Word. We do this because, when the Bible shows God creating, it doesn't show him doing it with tools, like a carpenter, but rather with words, like a magician. Christians, therefore, have gotten into the habit of talking about the Father's Eternal Word —the second Person of the Trinity—as the actual agent of creation. To put it all as briefly as possible, therefore: The Father *thinks up* a world, the Word *says* its name over the *brooding* of the Spirit, and presto, there you have a world.

Accordingly, when God says, "Let *us* make man in *our* image," it is specifically the image of the Trinity he has in mind. Furthermore, while man can be interpreted as being made in the image of all three Persons, it is especially fruitful to consider him as being made principally in the image of the Word—of the Son, the second Person of the Trinity. This seems legitimate for two reasons.

When God becomes man in Jesus, we always say it is the Word who becomes flesh, not the Father or the Spirit. On the principle that God doesn't change his mind, and in view of the fact that Jesus is what God finally says he had in mind for man, it seems fair to conclude that Jesus is what he had in mind all along. And since Jesus is the Word, that means that man had some special relationship to the Word from the beginning. Therefore, it does no violence to Scripture to interpret image as referring especially to the second Person of the Trinity.

Second, the account of creation in Genesis 2 tends to support this: "And out of the ground the LORD God formed every beast of the field, and every fowl of the air; and brought them unto Adam to see what he would call them: and whatsoever Adam called every living creature, that was the name thereof." *Naming* things is the crowning glory of man. Of the three operations of the mind—simple apprehension, judgment, reasoning—only one of them is distinctly and exclusively human; and it's the one most people guess last. It's not reasoning; monkeys can figure out how to put a fishing pole together in order to fetch bananas from outside their cage. And it's not judgment; my cat may not be able to predicate *mortality* of *man,* but he is definitely of the opinion that the *dried cat food* in his dish is *terrible*. No, the uniqueness of the human mind lies in simple apprehension—in our ability to form concepts, to extract essences, by means of words. Indeed, one of the best ways of thinking about what a concept is, is to conceive it analogically and call it an internal word or mental name. Accordingly, it is not farfetched to see our ability to name, to make words, as yet another intimation of our being made particularly in the image of the Word.

All right. The theological flashlight is sufficiently focused. Now point it at man and see what you can see.

Man, obviously, has dominion over the world. In earlier ages, this had to be taken largely on faith, because the world was so big and man was so small that there was not much evidence to prove he had the upper hand. To be sure, he arm-wrestled some forests into farms and some hillsides into building stones, but the minute he turned his back, nature started going her own willful way again.

In our time, however, the dominion of man over the world can be proved by unaided human reason. While the earth may still succeed in bucking us here and there for a while, it won't do it for long at the rate we're going. It's sad, of course, to have to prove it that way. It would be nicer if we, with all our present power, could point to a world which our dominion had loved into beauty and life. But it's quite enough, for the purposes of proof, to note that we have successfully converted most of the beauty and life it had into ugliness and death. And there is no doubt that we have the power to kill it off completely. And only a little doubt that we will.

Dominion, then. But how does our dominion over the world operate? What is its nature? Well, if man is in the image of the Word, perhaps it will be most fruitful if we see his power over creation as verbal power: For good or ill, we rule the earth by words.

Consider. Housebuilding was impossible until some man, somewhere, spoke a word. The human race was provided with no instinctive architectural faculties. The bees built hives, the birds made nests and the beavers worked like beavers, practicing housebuilding and stream control at the same time. But man built no houses until the day when one fellow who had sense enough to come in out of the rain sat down on a fallen tree he had dragged into his cave.

And it was so damp and dark and unpleasant that he got to thinking how wonderful it would be if he could arrange things so that he never saw the inside of a cave again. And as he thought, his eye fell on the tree on which he was sitting, and all of a sudden, an internal word sprang up noiselessly in his mind. He wasn't thinking the word *tree,* and he wasn't thinking the word *seat.* He was thinking a word he had never thought before. So he opened his mouth to hear what it was, and lo and behold, out came the word *lumber.*

It was such an odd word that he just sat there for a while. And all of a sudden, it happened again. Two new internal words in one day! Wait till his wife got home! But he couldn't wait, so he opened his mouth again and, this time, out came *house.*

Well, he was so enthused that he picked up the phone and dialed a friend.

"Irving?"

"Speaking."

"Irving, have I got news for you! You and I are going to make a bundle. You know that ax of yours? And all those trees you've got in that *yard* I thought up for you last week? You're going to split them up, and we're going to sell them for *lumber.*"

"For *what*?"

"No, Irving. Not for *what*. For *lumber*."

"What good is *lumber*? Who'd buy it? Nobody even knows what it is."

"Irving, Irving. Think big. When there's no market, you create one. We're going to sell the lumber to people who want *houses*."

"What's *houses*?"

"It's the plural of *house,* Irving. I just thought up both words this afternoon."

"What have you been smoking over there?"

"Nothing. I've just been thinking."

"That's even worse. Every time you think, I end up working."

"Believe me, Irving, this time you'll thank me. I've even got the name of our business picked out. In honor of your place, we'll call it The Lumber Yard. So hang up now and start chopping. I'm going to think up *writing* so I can letter the sign."

Obviously, it was a winning idea. And all the credit goes to the words of the earthly image of the Word. It is by words that we build. A house is a creature of words: stud, shoe, plate; king post, tie beam, ridgepole; jamb and lintel, mullion and meeting rail, board, batten, soffit and fascia. And houses themselves are called forth by words: Cape Cod, split-level, ranch; apartment, condominium, high-rise. It is words that turn houses into cities: street, avenue, plaza, park; dogcatcher, councilman, mayor, judge. And from the cities of men come those strange words—those renamings of creation and those namings of utterly new ways to name— which give the sciences the aweful power they have: acid, alkali, hydrogen ion concentration; diglycerides and butylated hydroxyanisole; trinitrotoluene, deuterium, and

U-235; indeterminacy, non-Euclidean geometry, entropy and curved space.

God's Word alone, of course, has the ultimate bark in it. When he says Be! there is nothing that has any choice but to jump. And when he hears his own eternal internal Word —when he knows all things in his dearly beloved Son— there is nothing that he doesn't know, no back part, no inner fold, no smallest speck at the heart of any smallest thing which that Word has left unspoken.

Our words do not have power like that. And yet, they have all the power we need, and more than we can handle. Not power enough to call things out of nothing, but enough to make Jerusalem of the world; not power enough to grasp things as they are, but power enough to wreck them as they stand.

In the beginning was the Word. . . . In the end, all it may take may be one word.

5
IMAGES

HAVING GOTTEN THIS FAR, I AM IN A POSITION
to deal with an objection I have been anticipating.

Many people are put off when they are exposed to theologians plying their trade. This refining of concepts, this
making of distinctions, this juggling of texts—it all seems
like a mere word game.

I concede every point—except one.

It all seems. . . . It does indeed. And on some days,
more so to theologians than anyone suspects. As a matter
of fact, the point could be made more strongly, and I would
still concede it. It doesn't just seem to be; it is:

A word game. No disagreement. Except to point out that
the same thing is true of every subject that ends in -ology,
and of a great many more that don't.

And that, of course, is why I finally draw the line at the
word *mere.* Word games are the least mere games of all.
They are power games; and the wise thing to do about them
is not to write them off, but to keep an eagle eye open whenever they are played. If you don't, you can lose a lot more
than your small change and your Scrabble set. You can lose
your way, your sanity, your money, or your life.

Accordingly, I overrule the objection as unfounded, and

27

go back to work investigating the peculiar power of theological language to shed light on the various projects which God and his creatures seem to have in mind.

Let me rather arbitrarily divide human speech into two categories: straight discourse and bent discourse; or, a bit more formally, into unrefractive and refractive uses of words. Straight discourse will cover all those uses in which words mean simply what they say. "Pass the salt," for example. Your mashed potatoes are too bland; you know salt will perk them up; you ask for it; and you get it. Everything is kept as literal as possible—and with excellent results. You can always count on words to sit still in this sort of discourse. No matter who uses it, the meanings remain the same.

Bent discourse, on the other hand, writes off this seeming advantage in favor of uses in which a single word may have several senses. *Analogy* has already been mentioned: It is perhaps the tamest, most disciplined sort of bent discourse. Here, however, I am interested in a far wilder and more fractious (or refractious!) way of talking: discourse by means of *images*.

"Pass the salt" got us salt and simplicity. "You are the salt of the earth" puts us in another ball game. We are now playing with *salt,* not as a word denoting a thing, a mere intellectual handle for moving odds and ends about. We are tossing around salt as an image. The word is no longer simply a grip on the outside of what salt does; it has become a probe into the mystery of what salt really is—both in itself, and in that dance of beings which we call creation.

Sharpen the distinction a bit. Calling it "a probe into the mystery" is slightly off the mark. Mystery is always inaccessible—by definition. What bent discourse actually does is take the word salt as an intellectual painting or icon. Then, on the basis of a firm belief in the power of words, it proceeds in one of two directions.

Sometimes it takes a very small corner of the painting and holds it up to view. For example: *Salt* perks up potatoes; life, unless it is perked up with a pinch of *bawdiness,* is flat and tasteless. Hence our hope (or our stuffy host's fear) that, with one more scotch, old Fred will let fly with some of his inimitably *salty* stories.

But at other, more important times, it takes the image, not by parts, but as a whole. It presents us, not with a detail of the painting, but with the entire word picture as an icon —as an almost holy sacrament, a powerful epiphany of all its meanings at once. The simplest, and perhaps the best, illustration is the image *Jerusalem.* Taken in its details, it can mean such things as the historical city, or the figurative hope of Israel, or the beloved of God, or the final destiny of creation. But used as an icon, it delivers all that freight of meaning in a single stroke. Take Blake's Jerusalem, for example:

> *I will not cease from mental fight,*
> *Nor shall my sword sleep in my hand,*
> *Till we have built Jerusalem*
> *In England's green and pleasant land.*

When you reach this level of refractive discourse, you have arrived at new heights of power. Straight discourse is potent enough: It delivers the goods, be they salt shakers or earth movers. But bent discourse is more powerful still, for it alone has light to shed on the Mystery which is our real home. True, it is inconvenient, volatile and inflammable. Straight words are like so many billets of firewood: They are useful, they may be stored with relative safety, and they do not spill or leak. Refractive words are more like tanks of high-octane gasoline, or reactors gone critical: They are much more useful, but a hundred times harder to handle —and they create hazards all over the place.

Nevertheless, the human race, at its wisest, has never hesitated to keep them in quantity and to pass them dangerously from hand to hand. Their inconvenience is put up with because of their glory. And their glory is precisely that they don't just lie there all safe and fireproof with a single meaning. Every time they change hands, their meaning grows more complex. Every icon is holy; but some icons have done more miracles and been handled by more saints, and therefore are holier than others. So with images: The more poets who handle them, and the more pentecosts of power they make in the minds of those who hear them, the greater their iconic power to hunt the Mystery itself.

One of the chief concerns of the theologian, therefore, must be an analysis of images. And not only of images themselves, but also of such general rules, if any, as he can formulate to ensure proper storage and handling of such potentially explosive material. This is particularly important nowadays because the education most of us have received has left us dangerously ignorant of how to think by means of images. Indeed, one of the reasons why the Bible is inaccessible to so many is that the Bible, at its deepest levels, is actually a tissue of images. The Word of God, when he most reveals himself, speaks with a bent tongue; if you have been brought up on nothing but straight talk and jargon, you will find him almost impossible to follow. Herewith, therefore, a few strictures on images, their use and their abuse.

Whenever you use an image, you will do well to think of yourself as standing in the middle of a plaza—one plaza among the many in the vast city of meaning that is human knowledge. Off this plaza run streets in many directions. These streets are the several distinct meanings to be found in the image itself. While you stand still in the plaza, you see all the streets at once; but if you decide to use the plaza as a way station to some other place in the city, you have to choose a street—a particular meaning—and follow it. Some of these streets will take you straight to your destination. But others will get you there only by detours—sometimes through the worst parts of town. Others still will turn out to be blind alleys with assassins lurking in dark corners. When you think by means of images, therefore—when you try to get somewhere in the city of meaning—choose your street carefully before you leave one plaza in search of another.

A simple illustration first. The relationship between the first and the second Persons of the Trinity is expressed in christian theology in terms of the image Father/Son. Take that as the plaza in which we stand. Now look around and see what streets lead off it.

Father/Son. Fathers come first; sons come second. Fathers are bigger; sons are smaller. Fathers and sons are not equal. How does that sound?

It sounds like a street which, if followed only a little further, would lead you straight into saying that the Father *made* the Son, and that the Son, therefore, isn't really God. But that's not where you want to go. You want to get to the plaza called God From God, Light From Light, True God From True God, located right at the end of One Substance Avenue. Look around for another way.

Father/Son. Fathers love sons; sons love fathers. Love between persons can be equal without having to be the same. Ah! That sounds more like it. That's a street worth taking. Off we go: Paternal love/Filial love—and so on.

If, on the other hand, you want an illustration of how taking the wrong street can cost you a lot of time, lead you through the gashouse district and almost get you mugged, turn to St. Paul's Epistle to the Romans, chapters 9 through 11.

Paul has been proceeding nicely through the city of his argument that we are saved, not by the Law of the Old Testament, but by Grace through faith in Christ. At the end of chapter 8, he has reached the beautiful plaza of Nothing Shall Be Able To Separate Us From The Love Of Christ.

Before going on to chapter 9, however, he formulates in his mind, but does not bother to express, a question which all of this raises: "If everything I have said so far is true, why is it that Israel—God's chosen people, the people with the true covenants, the true worship and the true promises —has rejected Christ?"

His goal is to arrive at the plaza marked out by Romans 11:26: And So All Israel Shall Be Saved. You and I, of course, would have no trouble at all getting there. We never walk the streets of the city of images if we can help it. We would call for a helicopter from Straight Talk Airways, Inc. and fly there. Our answer to the question would be the usual easy out: "Who knows why people do the things they do? Some Jews accept Christ; some don't. If God really is going to save all of Israel, then we'll have to trust God to work out the logistics."

It's a cagey answer, and it's a dull one, but for all that, it's not bad. It was unavailable to Paul, however, because he was an inveterate walker, a man for whom thinking in the images of the Scriptures was as natural as breathing.

So he starts out of Israel Plaza, down Abraham Street, gets to Jacob and Esau Place, and observes in passing that

God chose Jacob just out of mercy and rejected Esau just because he wanted to. He stands there awhile and asks the obvious question: "Is that fair?" He looks around, gets jittery and dashes down Moses Street to Pharaoh Square: God Hardens Whom He Will. He asks one more question: "Why does God blame anybody then? He's the only one responsible." And after that, he simply panics. He bolts down a side street and lands in a slightly seedy one-bench park at Isaiah 29:16, on the corner of Pot and Potter lanes: What Right Has The Pot To Talk Back To The Potter? From there, it's from bad to worse. His travels take him from Potter/pot to Vase/chamberpot: If God Wants To Make Israel The Recipient Of All The Shit He Can Dish Out, So What?

As you can see, Paul has arrived in Hell's Kitchen, talking like a native. Let us leave him there. He did, of course, eventually get where he was going, but by an even more tortuous circuit of images. Unfortunately, because he was writing Scripture, the net result of his labors was that he left behind a permanent record of the disastrous detour. And— alas—many Christians, failing to see the powerful logic of images at work, refused to see it as a detour: They made each step of his wandering way just as important as the goal, and built monumental theological constructions all over the passage—their ultimate achievement being the glorious doctrine of Double Predestination, which said that God put people in hell just for the fun of it.

It just goes to show you that if you insist on taking every-thing literally, you end up with some things you shouldn't take seriously.

6
WILLING

—WHICH BRINGS US TO AN INSTANCE IN
which all this advice can be put into practice.

Christians have carried on at length about the Will of
God, but they have often expounded the subject in ways
which were, if not as blatantly embarrassing as Double
Predestination, at least as inconvenient, uncomplimentary,
unscriptural and unbelievable. Has anything been said so
far that can raise the level of the discussion?

Go back, for a start, to our insistence that all discourse
about God is inevitably analogical: First of all, this forces
us to say clearly that we don't really know what we're talking about. Whatever it is in God that we're trying to char-
acterize by the word *will* remains a mystery. We must not
pretend that we can either know anything directly, or say
anything univocally about it. But second, in spite of all
that, the use of analogy allows us to insist that it is not only
legitimate but essential that we talk about the will of God.
If God acts at all, and if we are going to try to say anything
about his action, we're going to have to feature it to ourselves in terms of some faculty of our own. Will is simply
one of the highest analogues we have—right up there between knowledge and love. If any of our verbal tools can
do the job, will is bound to be among them.

But there is more than that to be said. The word *will* has
been around for quite a while. It long ago graduated from
the school of straight talk, if indeed it was ever in it. It may
not yet be the sacramental icon that Jerusalem has become, but it is nevertheless an image of considerable power.

Webster's Unabridged gives *will,* noun and verb, almost
two feet of fine print—and scatters its derivatives and com-
pounds over four additional columns. By any standard, that
makes a very large plaza of meaning, with a great many
avenues and streets (marked in upper- and lower-case letters) branching out on all sides.

Looking first at the southern, or warmer, side of the
plaza, we see DESIRE, WISH, DISPOSITION, INCLINATION,
APPETITE, PASSION and CHOICE. Off to the east run: Some-
thing Wished For, and REQUEST; off to the west: VOLITION,
A Disposition Manifested In Wishing, and The Collective
Desire Of A Group. And finally, on the colder, north side
lie SELF-CONTROL, SELF-DIRECTION, DETERMINATION, DE-
CREE, COMMAND, and Power To Control.

Now with a range of meaning like that, it makes a considerable difference which side of the plaza you take off
from. When I listen to some people talk about the will of
God, for example, I detect a preference for meanings which
lie on the northerly side. When they think of God as *willing,*
they seem to have in the back of their minds a collection of
images of a definitely austere sort. There is the king on his
throne issuing decrees right and left. There is the iron-
willed general determined to reduce the city to rubble. There
is the will power of the saint who touches no woman or wine
and gets up at the same ungodly hour every day.

It's all pretty stern stuff. Even when they talk about God's
will in milder terms, they still get in a coercive note. They
may say "God's will is simply what God wants," but you can

almost hear the unspoken "Or Else!" in the back of their
minds. It's as if they had been drilled in the old army rule
that a request from a superior is to be considered an order.
They never seem to escape from the area of power when
they expound will. More than that, the kind of power they
have in mind is usually conceived after the least human
model. Their saint's will power, for example, is thought of
as being most perfect when it brings him to the performance level of a machine. Fortunately, since they are usually
quite sensible people, the only damage this does is to per-
suade them to give that kind of religion a wide berth. Which
proves, I suppose, that a mistake isn't always a total loss.

No doubt this picture of will as coercive, as the ability to
Impose Patterns and Make Decisions Stick, strikes you as
more or less the traditional christian view. The church, perhaps, has seemed to you to have put into the words "the Will
of God" about the same tone as "Kinder, you vill all enjoy
your oatmeal—zis very minute!"

Admittedly, this preference for the more northerly, not
to say Prussian, meanings has been widespread; but for all
that, there is plenty of evidence in the tradition that the
streets on the southern side of the plaza have been well used.
Scholastic philosophy, for instance, defines *will* as "a rational appetite whose object is the good"—thus making
God's will a heavenly kind of appetite, a divine delectation.
Followed just a little further, that gives you a will of God
which, instead of being a chain of Divine Commands, is a
series of Divine Lip Smackings. And that, of course, is
nothing but what Genesis teaches on the subject: At the end
of each of the six days of creation, God says, *"Tov!"*—which
is Hebrew for "Mmm, good!"

I suggest, therefore, that if we want to get rid of some of
the unpleasantness that has crept into people's minds on the

subject of the will of God, we should work the southern side of the plaza. I suggest we pay less attention to the military-academy snapshots people have habitually been carrying in their wallets, and more to those pictures which show a little warmth and toastiness: namely, Inclination, Desire, Wish, Appetite, Passion and Choice. Let us make ourselves a promise to talk for a while about the will of God as attractive rather than coercive, as a delighting more than a deciding.

That done, the rest is easy. There is no contest for the most promising set of images to do the job. Having left the Square of Will via the Street of Desire, we land smack in one of the most gorgeous parts of the city—the Grand Plaza of The Song of Songs: love as the right way to read will; will as the desire of the lover for the beloved.

The will of God now becomes, not the orders of a superior directing what a subordinate must do, but the longing of a lover for what the beloved is. It is a desire, not for a performance, but for a person; a wish, not that the beloved will be obedient, but that she will be herself—the self that is already loved to distraction. The will of God, seen this way, is not *in order to* something, but *because of* someone.

For after all, only a fool of a lover ever tries to change the beloved; it is only after we have lost the thread of our love that we start giving orders and complaining about life styles. For as long as we follow it faithfully, it is always a matter of, "I could never have invented you, how should I know how to change you?" Outrage at the beloved is possible, of course. But in a wise lover, it is never outrage at anything but the beloved's destruction of herself. Inconvenience, pain, sleeplessness—even rejection—are nothing. The beloved is all.

That suggests, among other things, that the will of God

may well be, not *his* recipe for my life, but rather his delight in *my* recipe. It may well mean that he loves me in my independence, as any good lover would. Unfortunately, we have usually looked on the love of God for us as the love of a father for a small child. But that is not thoroughly scriptural. The grandest—and the final—imagery the Bible uses for his love is precisely that of lover and beloved, bridegroom and bride. It is the marriage of Christ and the church which is the last act of the long love affair between God and creation.

The love of father for child is the love of a complete being for one not yet complete. Even there, of course, the wise parent loves the child for himself, and never wills for a moment that the child remain a child. But the image is so colored by superiority/inferiority that it inevitably suggests that Doing What You're Told is what the lover really loves you for. Conformity, not independence, is the virtue it praises most. The lover's love for the beloved, on the other hand, suggests precisely the opposite. I think it is high time we took it seriously.

To illustrate: One of the difficulties in our thinking about the will of God has been caused by the crisis of change in the church. Everyone agrees, of course, that what we need most is To Do The Will Of God. The trouble is that very few people, unless they are faking it, know what the will of God for them is. There is a lot of pious talk about finding out about whether it is the will of God for you to marry Irving, or become a priest, or take the veil; but in all honesty, what you are really going to find out is what *your* will on the subject is, and whether you have enough nerve to go through with it. A few special types with inside tracks may get their answers straight from God, but the rest of us get them from ourselves—and from Irving, the Bishop and the Reverend

Mother, respectively. God is notoriously silent; and when he speaks, it is usually in parables, just so no one will be able to claim too much clarity and insight. He runs the world, not only with his hands in his pockets, but with his mouth mostly shut.

In the old days, this shortage of communications from God was compensated for by a very talkative church. Once you had made up your mind to marry Irving, the church could tell you, in burdensome detail, precisely what you would be doing: You would be getting up at 6:45 every morning without fail, cooking Irving's 4½-minute egg for precisely 4½ minutes, kissing Irving good-by, spending the day mopping up after Irving's children, having Irving's martini ready when he got home, feeding him his dinner, fetching him his slippers—and giving him a little action when he wanted it, no matter how deactivated you felt. And by doing all that, the church would assure you, you would be Doing The Will Of God.

Ditto Irving, if he decided to become a priest—except that he would tend to get less deactivated than you.

The trouble with such advice was that it paid so much attention to what was to be done, it neglected the person who was to do it. It forgot that The Will Of God For You included the word You. To be sure, you still celebrated your independence in theory, since it was you who freely chose to wipe all those dishes and bottoms; but in practice, you could hardly notice it.

In any case, however, times have changed, and we've all come a long way, Baby. Nowadays, if you insist, Irving can set his own alarm, boil his own eggs, and stir his own martinis. He may even, on some days, have it strongly suggested to him that he go activate himself. And you? God knows what you should do. But God isn't talking. And while the church may still be talking, it pretty obviously doesn't know. So we'll all just have to wait and watch as you do it. You and me both, in our inconvenient freedom.

And Irving? Well, I have been a parish priest for the past twenty-five years, and I wish him luck. It is the most unde-fined, ill-defined job on earth, and even the church is hardly pretending it knows what to say anymore. So he'll have to wing it, too.

We have, you see, been forced by change into a situation in which we are either going to have to stop talking about doing the will of God, or else find a way of seeing it in a new light. Specifically, we are going to have to find a way of seeing our now almost inevitable independence as the heart of our calling—of discovering that our present condition of flying by the seat of our pants may well be Doing The Will Of God.

And that is where The Song of Solomon comes to our rescue. The will, the desire of the lover is simply the beloved herself in her freedom: God just wants *us*. And the calling of the beloved is simply to love: The glory and the misery of the love affair is the master image for the understanding of our vocation. We are bidden, not to some fairy-tale mar-riage in which all is settled, but to a seeking and not finding, to the burning sense of loss in possession which only lovers know. "Tell me, O thou whom my soul loveth, where thou feedest . . . why should I be as one that turneth aside by the flocks of thy companions? . . . Stay me with flagons, comfort me with apples: for I am sick of love."

The will of God is not a list of stops for us to make to pick up mouthwash, razor blades and a pound of chopped chuck on the way home. It is his longing that we will take the risk of being nothing but ourselves, desperately in love. It is not a neatly arranged series of appointments in a tidy office, but a life of bad dreams, minor triumphs and major disasters—of things we did not have in mind at all, and of preoccupations that miss each other in the dark. "By night on my bed I sought him whom my soul loveth: I sought him, but I found him not. I will rise now, and go about the city. In the streets, and in the broad ways I will seek him whom my soul loveth: I sought him, but I found him not."

Might it not be, then, that it is by bearing for love the uncertainty of what we are to do that we come closest to his deepest will for us? In our fuss to succeed, to get a good grade on the series of tests we think he has proposed, we miss the main point of the affair: that we already are the beloved. We long ago wound God's clock for good. "Thou hast ravished my heart, my sister, my spouse; thou hast ravished my heart with one of thine eyes, with one chain of thy neck. . . . Thou art beautiful, O my love, as Tirzah, comely as Jerusalem, terrible as an army with banners."

It is our thirst for success and our fear of the freedom which he wills for us that keep us the poor lovers we are. If the cross teaches us anything, it should be that the cup doesn't pass from us, and that agony, bloody sweat, and the pain of being forsaken on a dark afternoon are the true marks of having said, Thy Will Be Done. He is no less lost in this affair than we are. What really matters for us both, though, is not the lostness, not the doubt, not the fragile, mortgaged substance of our house—only the love as strong as death which has set us as a seal upon each other's hearts.

7

FIGURING

THAT, OF COURSE, IS NOT INTENDED AS A full-blown treatise on the will of God. It is meant only to illustrate how a biblical flashlight of a warmer color might possibly illuminate our thoughts about a mystery we have come to find cold and forbidding. No doubt it creates more problems than it solves. But then, I never promised you answers.

Furthermore, it must not be allowed to give the impression that the butt of the theological enterprise is just talk about God. As a matter of fact, any christian theology that treated only, or even predominantly, of God would be, by just that much, untrue to the revelation. Theology is not, as the old manuals had it, "the science of God and things divine"; properly speaking, it is not about God, but about the mystery of God's relationship to the world. Accordingly, I want now to spend a little time refreshing some imagery which will get us out of an excessively "heavenly" perspective we may have sometimes had on the subject.

If you were to take a poll and ask the question "What is the Bible about?" the chances are you would get a majority of answers to the effect that it was about God, or about God's directions on how to get where God is. In other words, people would tend to think that the Scriptures are either

43

about spiritualities, or about a morality that leads to spiritualities. No doubt this is due in part to the fact that many people are simply ignorant of what is actually in the forbidding black book with the bowling alley down the middle of every page.

But for others, it is due to something more complicated. Many who have read the Bible—including some who know vast stretches of it by heart—hold the same overspiritualized view. Mere familiarity does not necessarily produce understanding. It is perfectly possible to know something (or someone!) all your life and still never really comprehend what you're dealing with. Like the Irishman in the old joke who received a brand-new toilet from his American cousins: He used the bowl for a foot washer, the lid for a breadboard, and the seat for a frame around the Pope's picture. Or less humorously, like the man who, when his wife of twenty years up and left him, wrote a long, sad piece in which he never once referred to her as a woman, or as a person, or by name.

Getting something right, you see, depends on more than just picking it up: You must also pick it up by the right handle. Accordingly, since the Bible consists entirely of words, that means picking it up by the right verbal handle —by the right set of images. And when you come at Scripture in that light, you quickly realize that no little shorthand intellectual formula like "spirituality" or "morality" will do.

First of all, the Bible refuses to tell you, in plain, simple words, what it is about. If you look for such capsule comment, you are bound to be mightily disappointed: The Scriptures, approached that way, seem only a potpourri of history, myth, poetry, prophecy and commentary. Second, when they finally do consent to tell you, they insist on using a profusion of images, types and figures to do the job—

which leaves almost as many unsatisfied customers as does its refusal to speak plainly. To be sure, they have a theme, and it is articulated by a logic of the most rigorous sort. But the logic is the logic of images and is unavailable to the literal-minded.

This is not to say that nothing in the Bible is literally true. Many things are, without any doubt. It is only to insist that, even when things are literally true, they still have to be interpreted by means of images before they yield their theme. Take the fact that Jesus ascended. Take it as literally true. The chief question still remains, So What?

At Hampstead, in the year 1562, a "monstrous pig" was born. So What?

Abraham, at the age of one hundred, had a son in Gerar, between Kadesh and Shur. So What?

Jesus floated up into a cloud from the top of a hill. So What?

It isn't until you start picking these things up by means of images that you can begin to differentiate and interpret them. It is only, for example, when the author of the Epistle to the Hebrews says that Jesus, in his ascension, is the Great High Priest entering into the Holy Place Not Made With Hands that the mere wonder of going up in the air like a balloon begins to yield a theme. The literal facts simply *are:* They don't mean a thing until you *figure* them.

There is an additional complication, however, when you come to deal with Scripture. The Bible makes up its own figures as it goes along. Events which at one point are mere events later become so loaded with meaning that they are used to interpret other events. When the Passover and the Exodus, for example, first occurred, they were just a miraculous escape act. But as the Jews carried those experiences with them through the wilderness and beyond, they came to use them as master devices for interpreting to themselves their unique calling to be the chosen people, the body of the Mystery. And when Christians looked around for a symbol with which to figure out what Christ's death and resurrection were all about, they picked up the Passover and the Exodus, too: "Christ our Passover is sacrificed for us," they sang at Easter; "therefore let us keep the feast."

This use of biblical events and persons as images, figures or types is called, appropriately enough, typology or typological interpretation; and it is essential to have some grounding in it, because the unity of the Scriptures can hardly be grasped without it. It is precisely by means of typology that this apparently random collection of books is seen as a single book with a single theme.

It is important, however, to make a sharp distinction between typology and mere allegory. Allegory is the symbolic expression, by means of fictional figures, of generalizations about human conduct. Bunyan's *Pilgrim's Progress* is a good example. The validity of allegory derives from the skill of the allegorizer; everything depends on how apt his figures are. Typology, on the other hand, does not involve making up arbitrary figures to illustrate already known generalizations; rather it involves picking up already given figures from one part of the revelation in order to interpret events in another part—events in which the same unknowable Mystery is at work. Its validity derives, not from the skill of the interpreter, but from a connection in reality between two events. To be sure, the connection is a theological one, and it is on the underside of the events, as it were; but it is taken as real nonetheless.

To illustrate: The Exodus is a type of the Resurrection of Jesus. This is so, not because I, or anyone else, finds it to be a kind of ready-to-hand allegory of some generality called deliverance or rescue, but because of the theological presumption that the God who acted in the Resurrection was the same as the God who acted in the Exodus—and because of the further presumption that, as the unique God he is, he has left some telltale marks of his style in both events. Both events, if you will, are manifestations of the same Mystery—fingerprints from the same hidden hand. The Exodus bears the print of God's little finger, perhaps, and the Resurrection of his thumb; they may be used together because they already are together.

Or, to change the illustration slightly: The Scriptures are the *Word* of God; you should expect, therefore, some persistent tone of voice to keep turning up. Detecting it, of course, will be largely a matter of having a good ear; but every now and then you can get, in different passages, nicely matching voiceprints. These are the antitypes; two different sets of words, two different conversations with the unseen caller; but a very clear impression of just Who is on the other end of the phone. That is how St. Paul comes to hold that the rock from which the children of Israel drank in the wilderness was none other than Christ—and why the compilers of the King James Bible took the liberty of sprinkling Christ's name all over the page headings of the Old Testament.

All right. Enough focusing of flashlights. Back to the question of the theme of Scripture.

If the Bible is not simply about generalizations like spirituality or morality, but about the Mystery of God's relationship to the world, what figure shall we use in order to grasp so elusive a theme? Well, on the assumption that almost all authors give themselves away in their last chapter, the choice is obvious. The image of images is Jerusalem, the City of God. Let us say, then, that the Bible is about the

Mystery by which God turns the world into the City; about how his sword does not sleep in his hand until he has built Jerusalem in the whole earth's green and pleasant land.

From that, the rest is easy. Herewith a cram course in the unity of the Scriptures.

8
COVENANTS

THE BIBLE PRESENTS US WITH THE MYSTERY
of God's work under two dispensations. It describes these
dispensations by means of the image of a covenant or testament between God and his chosen people. The Old Covenant, strictly speaking, runs from the receiving of the Law
by Moses on Mount Sinai to the birth of Christ; the New
Covenant, for all the remaining years of our Lord. If you
like references, the Old Covenant goes from Exodus 24
to Matthew 1; the New, from there on.

Before the making of the Old Covenant, however, three
preparatory covenants can be distinguished: one with
Adam, one with Noah, and one with Abraham. This makes
five covenants in all, and five great pivotal figures around
which the complex workings of Scripture are ordered into
a single engine of the Mystery: Adam, Noah, Abraham,
Moses, Jesus.

In each of these covenants, you can distinguish a demand, a promise, and a sign.

The *demand* is the same in all five, though the details
of it vary widely from one to another. For the sake of
simplicity, let us call it obedience: The demand of God is
that man should do his will.

The *promise,* too, is the same in all five. It is that the

City will be built, that the world will become Jerusalem—
or, in straighter language, that God's experiment of a free
creation will be a success after all. This promise, however,
appears in its fullness only when we come to the covenant
in Jesus; in the earlier ones, it manifests itself by degrees.

The *signs* of the various covenants all differ, but they
are by no means without a special unity of their own: When
they are interpreted typologically, they put on an electric,
mind-blowing display of theological arcs and short circuits.

I. THE COVENANT WITH ADAM

The demand for obedience is voiced affirmatively. Adam, like
all the rest of creation, is good. God tells him, "Be fruitful!
Multiply! Enjoy, enjoy! Dress and keep this hint of the
City, this garden I have given you, and make Jerusalem of
all the world." The tree of the knowledge of good and evil
is indeed set out; but only as the guarantee of the power of
Adam's freedom. The one negative demand is: "Leave *that*
alone. Don't do any funny, twisty things in your mind with
the good I have given you. Love creation for itself and for
the City, not for the mean things it can be made to mean."

The promise is that Jerusalem will indeed be built. "I
have given you everything. When you get it all named, it
will be a City you never dreamed of. And I'll help you.
When I walk in the garden in the cool of the day, we'll
chat about how things are going, and then have a Cinzano
and watch the sunset."

The sign is—well, you can take it a couple of ways. It's
the whole garden, seen as the hint of the City. Or it's the
Tree of Life in the midst of the garden. (Note—There are
two trees: one forbidden; one, presumably, allowed.) In

any case, both the garden and the tree are clearly signs of the covenant because, when the covenant is broken, both are withdrawn: Cherubim and a flaming sword are set at the east of the Garden of Eden to keep Adam from the openness and directness of his first calling. The City will still be built, but no longer straightforwardly—not any more in the simplicity with which an obedient Adam might once have raised it up. The Mystery of Jerusalem will work itself out now, not in straight lines, but by detours; not by intelligibilities, but by paradoxes and absurdities.

II. THE COVENANT WITH NOAH

The point of the story of Noah comes not at the beginning, but at the end. It is not that God destroys the world because of man's disobedience, but precisely that he forever renounces destruction as an answer to the problem of sin.

The demand, as before, is obedience. But this time the promise is that even disobedience won't stop the building of the City. This is the covenant of God's perpetual mercy. "I will not again curse the ground any more for man's sake. . . . While the earth remaineth, seedtime and harvest, and cold and heat, and summer and winter, and day and night shall not cease."

The sign of all this is the rainbow. "This is the token of the covenant which I make between me and you, and every living creature that is with you, for perpetual generations. I do set my bow in the cloud. . . . And I will remember my covenant . . . and the waters shall no more become a flood to destroy the earth." God unstrings his deadly bow of wrath and hangs it up forever on the wall of heaven. Or, if you like, he leaves it strung and points it, not at man, but at himself. In any case, this sign is not withdrawn: His mercy is forever. Sin is behovely; but all shall be well. All manner of thing shall be well.

III. THE COVENANT WITH ABRAHAM

Again, the demand is obedience; but this time, not to the sweet reasonableness of settling down in a garden and making a city of it. Now it is, "Get thee out of thy country, and from thy kindred, and from thy father's house, unto a land that I will show thee." Obedience has become absurd; only faith in the Mystery remains. The City is to be built by a pilgrim, on the run; Jerusalem will rise up among the non-existent children of a man too old to have any.

The promise, too, is refined: Not only will the City be built in an absurdity; it will be built in a scandal. It will not be raised up, even mysteriously, everywhere at once: The covenant is not with all men; it is only with Abraham's seed. But in that seed shall all the families of the earth be blessed. This is the covenant which specifies the means of the building of Jerusalem. In Adam, we saw the pure promise of the City; in Noah, the promise that it would be built in mercy; in Abraham, the promise that it will be built through a sacramental particularity, through a chosen people—through a church.

The sign? Circumcision. Forget the critics and their undoubtedly correct assertion that circumcision didn't really come into use until later. The author of Genesis puts it here as an interpretive device. Typology again. Only this time, read backward into the past, instead of forward into the future. The point is that the family of Abraham are the body of the Mystery. They are not a club of like-minded religious enthusiasts, or a learned society of Friends of Yahweh; they

are the vessel of God's purpose, marked in their flesh as the
place of the hiding of Jerusalem. "And ye shall circumcise
the flesh of your foreskin; and it shall be a token of the
covenant betwixt me and you."

IV. THE COVENANT WITH MOSES

The demand for obedience now takes the form of the Law
from Sinai. The Mystery, for a time, assumes the appearance of a plausibility: Do all these things, and you will
inherit the promise.

And the promise? It, too, seems to lose its absurdity: "If
thou shalt indeed . . . do all that I speak, I will be an
enemy unto thine enemies and an adversary unto thine ad-
versaries. . . . I will send hornets before thee, which shall
drive out the Hivite, the Canaanite, and the Hittite, before
thee. . . . And I will set thy bounds from the Red sea
even unto the sea of the Philistines, and from the desert
unto the river." It is the Promised Land: Jerusalem, not in
mystery, but in fact.

The sign is manifold. At first it is the Blood of the Covenant, sprinkled over the people at the reading of the Law.
But that is quickly overshadowed by the Ark of the Covenant, the sacred box in which the Tables of the Law were
carried, and over which, between the cherubim, dwelt
Yahweh, God of Israel, whom the heaven of heavens could
not contain, but who, himself a pilgrim, deigned to pitch
his tent among his people. And therefore, the Tent—the
Tabernacle, the portable temple in which the Ark was kept
in the Holy of Holies—becomes part of the sign, too. And
so, eventually, does the Temple at Jerusalem which replaced
the Tabernacle when the wanderings were over.

And yet. The wanderings never really ended. A pilgrim

God demanded a pilgrim people. The absurdity only seemed to depart. Jerusalem became an intelligibility only for a time: David, Solomon. That was about the extent of the glory. From there on, it was all downhill—a deeper descent into the Mystery than ever before. The kingdom divided; Jerusalem destroyed; her people led captive to Babylon. Ten centuries of the gradual defeat of every plausible hope; a whole history of being run over by every steamroller in the ancient world: Damascus, Nineveh, Egypt, Babylon, Persia, Greece, Rome. The Old Covenant still intact, but the only constant sign—the Blood of Israel itself: the Suffering Servant of Yahweh.

V. THE NEW COVENANT IN THE BLOOD OF JESUS

The demand takes its final form: It is obedience, not to the Law, but to Grace by faith; to the ultimate absurdity of a God who gives Jerusalem for free.

The promise: New Jerusalem. A new heaven and a new earth. The holy City, prepared as a bride adorned for her husband. Twelve gates, twelve foundations. A street of pure gold, transparent as glass . . .

And the sign? The Blood of Jesus, the Blood of the New Covenant. More fully, the Sacred Humanity of Jesus himself . . .

I stop there, however. When imagery reaches that point, it becomes a critical mass. I want to save the fireworks of the ultimate explosion for the end.

9
PRIESTHOOD

WE HAVE BEEN TALKING SO FAR ABOUT THE images with which we hunt the Mystery—about gardens and cities, covenants and blood. Time now to talk a little about the actual object of the hunt: about the habits and habitat of the Mystery itself.

All this discourse on the building of Jerusalem through covenants raises the question of the nature and extent of the operation. To begin with: Is it all an afterthought? Are the covenants merely adventitious—a supervening tidying up of a chaos which would never have become order without them? Are they extraneous transactions aimed at making a city of a world which is fundamentally alien to becoming one?

The answer appears to be no. The Mystery of the City enters at the beginning, not later on: The Garden is Jerusalem in the bud; Adam is the agent of the City from the start. At the very least, it seems better to view the history of the covenants as a long effort to get the original show back on the road—as an attempt to get Adam's agency back in business, so that the citifying of the world can go forward as intended.

But that raises a further question: Is Adam—is man—the only city builder? Does the world, apart from him, have

55

no citifying tendencies? Or does the working of the Mystery go deeper? Does it lie, perhaps, at the very roots of all creation? And if so, how does it work in the orders below man? What images do we have which will shed light on cities which hide in the wordless dark?

Enough. That should keep us busy for a while.

Theology, as I said, starts from the top. When a theologian wants to find out something about man, he begins at Christ, and works his way down by a series of analogical and sacramental handholds. Watch.

Jesus is Perfect Man. He is what God always had in mind for humanity and finally succeeded in getting. What is true of his human nature, therefore, will be a sacramental showing forth of what is true of all men. Accordingly, if Jesus is the Great High Priest—the offerer of creation to the Father, the reconciler of the world to God—all men may fruitfully be understood to be, in some sense, priests, offerers, reconcilers.

Thus the Priesthood of Christ, the Mystery which he sacramentalizes when he at last ascends into the Holy Place Not Made With Hands, becomes the key to the very first thing that Adam does when God breathes into his nostrils the breath of life: He offers, he reconciles, he lifts creation into ever higher unities. Adam, therefore, may be viewed as a priest: He offers the garden into the City; he names the beasts into an animal kingdom which they, unreconciled and speechless, could never know; he lifts the common coupling of the world into the mystical union of marriage.

Moreover, having come that far with this interpretive device, you can even run it backward: The priesthood which Jesus shows forth at the end is simply the priesthood which Adam had at the beginning, brought to its proper functioning. This, you will note, is the same device by which

St. Paul calls Christ The Last Adam. Some people dislike it, because they see it as a case of circular reasoning—of assuming what you started out to prove, and then using the results as proof of your assumption. But those are the people who fail to see that word games, especially image games, are also understanding games, reflection games. The flashlight shines in the mirror and the mirror shines back at the flashlight. The exercise doesn't create any new light, but it really does shed light where there wasn't light before. In both directions.

Accordingly, I shall make another unprovable assumption and go straight to work. I raised the question whether the creatures below man—the lower orders, as we sometimes snobbishly call them—can be better understood if we see them, too, as involved in the working out of the Mystery of the City on their own level. I shall assume that the answer is yes. And I shall further assume that, just as the light of Christ can legitimately be pointed at man, so the reflection of that light can be bounced from man to animals, vegetables and minerals—for fun and profit.

To a degree, indeed, I have already done so. When I ended up in chapter two with a sunflower which knew where the sun was, I got there by predicating a human faculty, knowing, of whatever unknowable thing it was that the sunflower was really doing. I justified it then by saying that, since all discourse about beings other than ourselves is heavily analogical anyway, we might as well use de luxe analogues. On that same principle, I want now to take an even more de luxe analogue and predicate it of the lower orders—an analogue taken this time, not from philosophy, as knowledge was, but from the symbols of revelation. I propose to try the image of *priesthood* on the idea of *evolution* and see if it fits.

One slight further justification to get us going. From a theological point of view, there are reasons to expect this to be valid. When we say man is made in the image of God, we immediately open the door to saying that other creatures than man may well be in the image of God, too. Three lines of reasoning lead to that conclusion.

First, earlier theologians held that the image of God in man was evidenced by man's possession of knowledge and free will (as symbolized in Genesis by the naming of the animals and the command not to eat the forbidden fruit). If you take that stand, however, it is plain that knowledge and will exist below man—at the minimum, in most of the animal order and possibly also in the vegetable. Man, accordingly, should not be viewed as a lonely sketch of God tucked into a book full of meaningless scribbles. Rather he should be seen as the best self-portrait in a whole exhibition of self-portraits. Everything in the world looks like God, to one degree or another.

Second, even if you come at the image of God in man as more recent theologians have, you get the same result. They locate it by means of such phenomena as love and sexuality: To be made in the image of God means to be made in the image of the Trinity; accordingly, man's inveterate mutuality is the visible evidence of the Mystery. Again, however, man is not all alone making love in the upstairs bedroom of the world; there's a lot of sex going on in the basement: "Birds do it, bees do it, even educated fleas do it." Ergo, et cetera.

Finally, if you take the image of God in man as referring preeminently to the image of the Word, the second Person of the Trinity, you arrive once more at the same point. The Word, in the solemn interchanges of the Trinity, is the one who offers creation to the Father—he is a priest forever;

not just since the incarnation, but before all worlds. Man, therefore—Adam, from the word go—is a priest. But the priest business cannot be limited to man, any more than the love business can. The world is full of little shops and cottage industries going full tilt at the work of offering up. Furry bodies lifting vegetable cells into animal tissue; tomato plants lifting mineral matter into vegetable stuff; even, this time, minerals strangely lifting themselves into shape: the formation of crystals is pretty odd, if you think about it for a while.

Priesthood, therefore, may not be a bad image at all with which to tackle the question of why this is an evolutionary world. At the very least, it ought to be given a try, because the images which modern thinkers have been using on the subject are, all of them, grossly unsatisfactory.

Consider the various explanations which have been handed us. They fall into two categories: chance theories and program theories. The chance theory is worthless as an explanation, because chance never explains why an individual event happens—it only describes the general pattern of events. My insurance company bases my premiums and its profits on the statistical certainty that not more than x forty-eight-year-old males will die in a given year. I take some comfort from the fact that this enables the Prudential to come to my wife's rescue in the event of my sudden demise. But I learn nothing from it about the possible causes of my death; such as, for example, a little conspiracy between her and the Prudential man to put prussic acid in my birthday box of marzipan.

The chance theory does have one virtue, however. By the very fact that it does not explain the individual steps of evolution, it at least leaves room for the idea that, somehow, individual things really act on their own, even when they take an evolutionary flyer. It leaves a place in our philosophy for the concept of a radically free creation.

It is precisely the denial of the real and obvious freedom of everything to act for itself—and the transfer of the agency of evolution to a bunch of strong-arming theoretical spooks—that makes the *program* theories so unacceptable. It doesn't matter which one you take. They all come to the same fundamentally unbelievable conclusion, namely, that the whole history of the growth and development of the world was predetermined. The secularist version says that it was determined by an unbreakable chain of causes and effects: From the dawn of creation, everything had to happen the way it did because the material sequence of causes simply had to go the way it did. That, obviously, is not a scientific theory, but a philosophical article of faith. It is not so much an explanation as a bald assertion. If it has any advantage, it is that it so plainly explains nothing that only a believer can hold it.

The religious version of the program theory, however, is even worse. It is indeed an explanation, and a great ham-handed divine one at that. It does, as the secularist theory does not, assign a sufficient cause for the programing: If God isn't enough, then nothing is. But when you say that God predetermined the entire natural history of the world and punched the program into some kind of built-in computer, your explanation hits the bull's-eye—but on the wrong target. You explain the world perfectly. Only it's not this world you explain; it's one you made up in your head.

In your world, my dog pees on the second lamppost from the corner because he could not, in the nature of reality as programed by God from all eternity, do anything else but pee then and there, in full and on time. In this world— and, admittedly, I mean my world—my dog pees where he damn well pleases. And the weeds in my garden grow where they damn well please. And the tree that fell and broke my fence fell where it damn well pleased. And I have damn well damned all three of them. Because the hallmark of a free world is every sane thing's deep inner conviction that it is metaphysically proper, practically useful and socially acceptable to give a damn. God does. I do. And so does my dog, if you catch him in a foul mood. So compute me no computers, secular or divine. I'll bet you my world against yours any day in the week.

One more thing. The program explanations of evolution all have an unexpressed common assumption which ought to be damned while we're at it. It is that if, by any chance, you could manage to do the history of creation over, you would get the same result. Of course, no one ever will, so the assumption is safe from having to pass any experimental test. But haven't they learned anything from the tests they have done? They have been breeding fruit flies for decades now, and they have gotten some pretty bizarre fruit flies in the process—but nothing much besides fruit flies. That doesn't speak very well for their penchant for plastering philosophical necessity all over the upward thrust of the evolutionary process. Why doesn't it occur to them that maybe there never was any obligation to evolve? Desire is just as respectable a philosophical concept as necessity. Why don't they try that on for size? My theory is that when, as and if the fruit flies decide to put on an evolutionary spectacle, they're not going to pull out of the barrel some script they used the first time around. They'll just wing it.

Because the world is, mercifully, not TV. There never has been a rerun and there never will be. Even things that repeat themselves don't repeat themselves: Today's sunrise is not yesterday's—and today's sun itself is just a wee bit colder, one small step further along the road to the home for retired stars. The world is not a film which can be re-run; it is a single impromptu performance, a piece of street theater by a pickup company who never saw each other before or since, who did what they did, tossed off whatever lines came into their heads, barged into each other, punched each other, kicked and bit, or kissed and made up, as it seemed convenient at the time—and closed to rave reviews with a rousing improvisation of *New Jerusalem* that made everyone go shivery all over.

You see? That makes a better world. Evolution as a fact is fair game. So is the investigation of the physical mechanisms by which it operates. But evolution explained as a philosophical necessity is malarkey. The explanation is either worthless or dreadful—or else it's a dodge to avoid talking about history. Which is even worse, because history is the real key to the subject after all.

We used to go at it that way. We used to talk about natural history. History was a nice high-class, human ana-logue, and it made for a sensible view of the world. But then we got into the habit of using the neutral word evolu-tion and interpreting it—*figuring* it—by means of subhu-man images. We filled our heads with pictures of machines and computers. And, inevitably, we blew it.

Let's go back, then, and talk history. In one sense, his-tory can be taken as nothing more than chronicle: the bare sum of all the interactions of persons and things from the beginning of time. But in the most important sense, history is not an attempt to record everything; it is a quest to dis-cover, by means of words and images, a shape in the course of time—to figure the Why and How of events. And when you come to that task, you do it badly if you attempt it by talking about external or internal forces. You do it well

only if you use more elevated and uplifting language—only
if you try to see the shape of events as due to the character
of the various and several participants, human and nonhuman alike.

It was, for example, because of the relentlessly alpine
character of the Alps—and the so remorselessly hannibalis-
tic nature of Hannibal—that the world got the particular
war movie which those two collaborated to produce. Without the unique actions which freely flowed from their dis-
tinctive characters, it would have been another picture:
It was characteristic of Hannibal to *think big,* but to be,
regrettably, *unable to fly.* It was characteristic of alpine
passes to have *fresh snow* on top of *old ice* in October. Put
the two together and you get lots of scenes with sliding
elephants. There was, however, no danger of getting another picture. What was, was; what might have been just
wasn't. The history we got is the result of all the characters
who were mixed up in it. If you are serious about asking
Why and How, you will just have to study character.

Which is where priesthood comes in. In trying to figure
an evolutionary world—to find an image which will shed
light on the reason for evolution—we need something which
will be characteristic of every creature in the process. For
this is a very peculiar world. By all odds, it should, like
everything else in the universe, be running downhill toward
absolute zero. Indeed, like everything else, it is. Why then
is its most obvious historical characteristic the glorious
evolutionary march uphill? Why the boats-against-the-cur-
rent theme over and over again? Why, in the face of
entropy—in a universe in which the ultimate degradation
of matter and energy leads to a state of inert uniformity of
component elements, to the absence of form, pattern, hier-
archy or differentiation—why, in the face of all that, is the

story of the world always more differentiation, greater hierarchies, splashier patterns, more gorgeous forms? Why does the nicely uniform primeval slime end up less uniform? Why ants in the hill? Why bees in the hive? Why stags fighting in the plain for the leadership of the herd? Why men who would run over their grandmothers to get somebody elected President? Why? Why? Why?

Well, I suggest that it is because, in some sense, everything in the world, every man jack of the cast of billions involved in this piece of improvisational theater we call history, is a priest. God has built into everything he made, not a tape obedient to an external programer, but a bent for offering on its own, a yen to lift for itself, an insane craving to make things more complicated just for the personal pleasure of doing so. Everything that hangs around this crazy performance watches like a hawk for a chance to make its move of offering up. On most days, it does its offering within the ordinary limits of its present nature. Ants offer up sand into anthills, bees lift nectar into honeycombs, and little slimy things do their thing with the slime. But on those rare days when the out of the ordinary happens, when, as a result of something fairly jazzy, things change—when there is an increase of radiation due to a storm on the sun, and a funny thing happens to somebody's DNA on the way to the theater—then that somebody doesn't just stand there. Like a running back looking for a break in the line, he shouts, "Light!" and tears through. He moves out, not because he was programed to do so by some coach but because he knows in his bones the object of the game—and, on his own, he makes his move.

Last step. Since all the running backs in creation are priests, the name of the game is offering, lifting, moving things up. That, I think, is what Teilhard de Chardin was saying, at least if you interpret his omega point as the target I believe he meant it to be. In any case, it makes more sense than determinism. It leaves you with Christ the Offerer *out there* as the goal of creation, and with Christ the Offerer *in here* making everything in his priestly image so that nothing fails to know the object of the game. Best of all, it leaves you with every single thing, top to bottom, free to play.

10
COMPUTERS

USING THE IMAGE OF PRIESTHOOD TO ILLU-
minate the concept of evolution shows how good images
can protect us from being robbed of our heritage of mystery
and, incidentally, keep us from solemnly mouthing a lot of
sillies. But there are bad uses of images, too. The power of
words is such that they can do nasty things. A horrible
example is in order.

Consider the love affair which modern man is currently
carrying on with the computer. It is a perfect instance of
how we get in dutch philosophically. Note, first of all, that
I am not talking about computers as such. From the abacus
on up to tomorrow's generation of supersophisticated elec-
tronic jobs, they are useful gadgets. I am talking here
about what we think of the computer—about the way the
image of the computer has developed in our minds, and
how we have done ourselves a philosophical mischief with
it.

The abacus seems not to have been much of a problem.
People simply used it and let it go at that. They didn't turn
it into an image and apply it to themselves. Nobody said
admiringly that young Sneed had a mind like an abacus—
probably because they knew the remark would be used as a
straight line for: "Too bad he's lost half his marbles." Back

67

in those days Sneed Junior would most likely have been
complimented for having a mind like a steel trap.

The hand-operated adding machine was no problem
either. Like the abacus, it worked at roughly human speed;
no one was seriously tempted to look up to it, or to figure
out the mysteries of human nature by means of it. However, with the introduction of electrical and, later on, elec-
tronic machines, trouble began to brew. The computer acquired the virtue of speed. Sneed Secundus took it kindly
when the Boss told him he had a brain like an adding
machine.

But then, things went even further. The manufacturer
added information storage and retrieval capacity to his
already speedy piece of hardware. The Boss found himself
tempted to transfer his compliments from Sneed to the
machine. He praised it for its marvelous *memory* and for
its ability to *figure things out*. He said it *thought* more
clearly than Sneed, and in a final, idolatrous burst of enthusiasm, he punched in gossip about his political enemies
and rubbed his hands in glee, because now it *knew* which
senators liked boys better than girls.

But notice how things are getting badly out of control.
On several fronts. For one thing, the reductionist fallacy
is on the attack: We have substituted brain for mind—the
instrument by which we know for the *faculty* of knowing.
This has been done for so long now that "brains" is simply
common speech for "intellect." "But," you say, "what's so
dangerous about that? It's no different than substituting
'heart' for various functions of the will, as in 'have a heart,'
meaning be merciful, or 'miles and miles of heart,' meaning
very sympathetic."

Don't kid yourself. Heart is an old giant among images;
it's big enough to handle mystery with some resourceful-
ness. Brains is a midget—and a latecomer to boot. It is

dangerous because you can't make an image of something that minor—with so little accumulated iconic content—without beefing it up a bit. Unfortunately for us, by the time brains was common usage, the most tempting image we had to figure it with was, lo and behold, the computer. Consequently, we started tossing off lines like "the brain is nothing but a computer made of meat"—which is reductionism rampant, nothing-buttery *in excelsis.*

But that wasn't all. Besides replacing mind with brain and brain with computer, we also lost track of which operations of the intellect came first. We substituted *thinking* for *knowing.* In spite of the fact that for ages we had them in the right order (1. simple apprehension; 2. judging; 3. reasoning), we carelessly talked ourselves into substituting the last for the first. "I think so" used to run a weak second to "I know so," but we spent so much time prattling on about reasoning as the principal ornament of man's mind that we lost the ear for the distinction.

The sad thing about such confusion of tongue is that it leads straight to confusion of face: It leads us into the reductionist's hall of mirrors where we can no longer see ourselves as we really are. We take the fact that many animals obviously think, and the fact that the thinking of some of them comes amazingly close to reasoning, and we jump to the fanciful conclusion that human thinking is nothing but a special case of animal thinking—which means, of course, that it's nothing very special at all. Obviously, then, when somebody produces a machine that can reason circles around people, we are sitting ducks for the ultimate folly: We seriously begin to think about resigning our membership in The Animal and Vegetable Country Club and joining the Mineral Chowder and Marching Society.

Of course, our disgrace is entirely our own fault. Because the one thing the computer doesn't do is *know*. "Ah, but just a minute," you say with a wicked gleam in your eye. "This time I've got you. Why can't I say the computer knows? *Knowing* is simply an analogue. You applied it to sunflowers; why can't I slap it on the IBM System/370?"

You have a point. Knowing is indeed an analogue; and you may, if you like, predicate it of a machine. As a matter of fact, I want to reserve myself the right to predicate it, in some sense, of everything—all the way down to the bottom of the mineral kingdom. What you are forgetting, however, is that people who say the computer knows, and then proceed, on a reductionist basis, to attack the uniqueness of human knowing are, by definition, using the word, not analogically, but univocally. Analogy is a way of shedding light on things that are really different, but alike in some respect. It predicates the concept *knowing* of both man and computer, but it never kids itself for a moment that it means the same thing in both cases. Univocity also predicates a single concept of two different things, but it does so in exactly the same sense: *Black* is the night; *black* is the color of my true love's hair. Clearly, since reductionists always end up saying that man is nothing but a computer, they are not using analogy at all. They are really no better than the old lady who believes that her cat actually conceptualizes the way she does. The only difference is that she pays the cat an undue compliment, while they give man a nasty slur.

But that's not all. Even a good analogue, used with due respect for the rules of analogy, has to be handled with discretion. I am obviously in favor of great boldness in this matter, especially after the last chapter, in which I set myself up for the job of explaining what in the world the priesthood of oysters and stones could possibly be. But a little prudence never hurts. Remember, when you apply an image to something, you release iconic power in both directions. To be sure, shining the light of knowing on the computer mightily enhances the computer. It takes the word a giant step closer to becoming an icon in its own right. But by that very fact, the computer now has power to reflect *its* light on knowing. And that's where trouble can start. Unless you keep careful track of which was the prime analogate, you may wind up rubbing mother nature the wrong way.

For after all, there is a hierarchical grain to these things. Witness: I *know*. And my dog *knows*. And the lobster *knows*. And the sunflower *knows,* and the stone *knows.* . . . But as you go further down the ladder, you run an ever-increasing risk of charley-horsing the long arm of analogy. The predicate takes a much safer hold at the top than at the bottom.

That is why I am reluctant to predicate *knowing* of a computer. It's a collection of mainly mineral junk. It's not even as far up the ladder as rutabaga: It's a machine, not an organism. (There's another pair of images that have been used in the same reductionist way. "Your body is a machine; fuel up with Chaff Flinkies for breakfast!") Organism, not machine, is the prime analogate; the machine is made in the image of the organism, not vice versa. For my money, I'm even prepared to say that a sunflower knows better than a computer. Not knows more; knows better. For when we use the phrase "it knows," we refer at least as much to the *it*— to the unique "selflike" quality which is the hallmark of an organism—as we do to the operation of knowing. The computer "contains" knowledge, perhaps, and can be programed to follow the steps of the thinking process; but what does the computer itself know? What does *it* think? Does it have any self-consciousness, any personal convictions? Does it have a heart? Even an eighth of an inch of one? *Chat fance,* as they say in French. And if you don't believe me, wait till the tender mercies of the IRS computer catch up with you. Instant conversion.

One of the tests that should regularly be applied to the results of any thinking process, however plausible, is: Would I like to sit down and have a vermouth with this thing I have just talked myself into? On that scale, ballerinas, oysters, free speech, and romantic love come off just fine. Computers, the Modern Presidency, National Honor, Protective Reaction and Keeping America Number One make terrible drinking companions.

A man is not only known by the company he keeps, he is influenced by it. Evil communications corrupt good manners. And if all your communication is with nothing-butters, the corruption doesn't stop at bad manners. You yourself become frequently bad, usually sad, and almost invariably, mad. Bad, because the root of all sin is the perversion of the priesthood by which we offer the world into the City. That *civilizing* priesthood is, as I said, principally verbal. The longer you persist in saying that things are not what they are—that man is not a human being but a computer, that the computer is not a piece of hardware but a god—the more you are tempted to make wicked and uncivilized offerings. To do bad things long before you yourself have become a bad man.

People profess to wonder how men with such nice tailors, barbers and family lives could become a plague of Water-buggers. They don't seem to understand evil. They expect horns, hooves and the gestures of blatant villainy; but that's not the way it works. With evil, in a classic paradigm of perversion, the beginning is in the word: It starts with the verbal abuse of reality. Adam sinned after Eve said that the tree was something to be desired to make one wise. We got Watergate and the secret bombing of Cambodia after we got NASAspeak and Nixonese—after the Pentagon abolished foursquare talk. Not that we weren't warned: "The tongue is a fire, a world of iniquity. . . ." No man can tame it. "It is an unruly evil, full of deadly poison."

But besides making you bad, it makes you sad. There you stand, next to a computer which you know is less than you, but which you have come to think knows more than you. Apart from accidents, the thing that makes people sick or well, glad or sad, is their own deepest belief about themselves. Shame came into the world only after Adam thought he was naked, sadness enters when he—the *dominus mundi,* the lord of this world—ceases to believe in his own kingship. Even an oyster gets sad when he loses his religion. How much sadder, then, must it make a man when he talks himself into thinking he is just a little punk, no better than a machine?

Sad enough to make him mad. Angry mad, because he has been robbed of something precious and has so tied the hands of his mind that he can't get it back. Crazy mad, because angry men are dangerous, and always do something when they can't do the right thing. And finally, stark staring bonkers mad, because he has reached behind his back, picked himself up by his belt, held himself over his own head, and is now occupied with the problem of how to change hands.

The Word always creates. And words always create. The idiot, by definition, is simply a man who has talked himself into a world of his own.

11
SOULS

IT SHOULD BE NOTED, HOWEVER, THAT THE mischief done by the creative power of words is not always the result of such wretched usages as the one in the last chapter. Some of it comes from the mishandling of perfectly good words and images.

One of the ground rules of all thinking, especially in philosophy and theology, is that no one gets very far unless he is willing and able to make distinctions. There are times when my first-year theology course turns into one long harangue on the theme "If you don't distinguish, you can't theologize." After all, reality is a mystery inaccessible to our minds. You can't form a concept of existence; you can only affirm or deny existence of some known essence: Horses *exist,* are real beings; centaurs *do not exist,* they are only mental beings. What our minds deal with directly are *essences*—the intelligibilities *by which* we grasp the act of being. We should regularly expect, therefore, that a great deal of refining and distinguishing of concepts will be necessary before we arrive at the best mental grasp of things in hand.

Do you see how inevitable it is? The last two paragraphs contain six distinctions, tossed in without half trying: Wretched Usage/Good Usage; Good Usage Well Handled/

Good Usage Mishandled; Mystery/Intelligibility; Existence/
Essence; Real Being/Mental Being; and for the boys in the
philosophical back room, a hint of the distinction within
essence between *id quod est,* and *id quo est quod est.*

But for all its inevitability, it takes a heap of handling to
keep the distinguishing business from driving you out of
house and home. If you can bear with just one more distinction, our distinctions themselves can bankrupt thought in
two ways: by defect or by excess. *Sex* is a good example of
a concept practically in the poorhouse by reason of a de-
ficiency of distinction. Originally it referred to gender: We
distinguished in human nature two sexes, male and female.
But in modern times, that usage has been almost completely
papered over. Sex has come to refer, not to the distinction
between two things, but to some third thing which is the
same for both sexes—or, worse yet, to anything done, alone
or with others, involving the physical organs by virtue of
which the distinction was first noticed. The very word,
therefore, which was supposed to be a sharp probe to explore the full range of the mystery of humanity as male and
female, becomes a dull tool which, more often than not,
obliterates the distinction altogether. Thus the barbarisms
which go unnoticed every day: "I wish I had a sex life"; "Sex
without fear"; and "Lose weight through sex." And thus,
too, the old chestnuts which, to do them credit, at least have
the sense to poke fun at it: "Name: EVELYN SNEED; Age:
23; Sex: OCCASIONALLY." And the one about the fellow who
came into the office looking for Sexauer: "*Sexauer!* We don't
even get a coffee break!"

Abuse of distinction by defect, however, is often small
potatoes compared to abuse by excess. Take a simple illustration first.

When we set about to do justice to what is distinctively

human about man, we frequently try to pick up that mystery by means of a distinction between knowledge and will. We discern in ourselves not only a consciousness of *what* we are doing, but also an ability to decide *that* we will do it. Every human act, of course, is a seamless whole: Even if I just sit around and know, I nevertheless will to do it; and if I will to do something, it always has to be something I know. Nevertheless, the distinction has been with us right from the beginning—and it served us well, as long as it wasn't pushed to the point of talking about knowledge and will as if they were separate departments sending interoffice memos to each other. For there is no such *thing* as knowing, no such *thing* as willing. The only *thing* in actual being is man— and we do our thing as wholes, not by parts.

The temptation to excess, therefore, comes in the form of a penchant for thinking of the two parts of a mental distinction as if they were separable and actually existing things. It is a temptation to let the creative power of words get out of hand—to allow the terms to *reify* themselves and act as if they had a life of their own. To some extent, of course, this is inevitable. But it is safe only if you continually remember the original purpose for which the distinction was made, namely, the competent handling of a mysterious wholeness.

Which brings me to a larger and more theological illustration: the distinction we make between *body* and *soul* when we talk about man. Faithful to my general rule, I shall try first to find out what led the human race to talk about body/soul to begin with.

Adam, in his undoubted exhilaration at having successfully named all the animals, probably imagined for a while that his naming days were over. He was wrong. We have already seen his son the cave man, naming away on level

after level. But even before the tour de force which gave
Irving so much trouble, Adam came up against a problem.

He has, let us say, named the following things: Meadow;
Large Tree Standing Alone In Midst Of Meadow; Cow. But
then he comes up against his first Thunderstorm. Ever con-
scious of his priestly duties, he promptly names Rain and
Lightning. Cow, obedient to the more limited dictates of her
nature, proceeds to take refuge under Tree. Lightning strikes
Tree and bowls over Cow. When Rain stops, Adam goes
over to Cow and puts his verbal priesthood to work again.

He looks at the beast lying on the ground. At first it seems
to be the same Cow he named last week—and which, only
two nights ago, he learned to call Sleeping Cow. But then
he begins to notice differences: no motion at all; no breathing. "Thunder and grindstones!," he cries. "A Dead Cow!"
He puzzles for a while over the cause of this change and
finally concludes that, since no more breath is coming out
of Cow, she must simply have run out of breath.

So he fetches his bicycle pump and tries to give her a refill. No good. Maybe she needs real breath instead of air. He
tries mouth-to-mouth resuscitation. Again no good. Maybe
she's just got a vapor lock: He jumps on her ribs with both
feet. A little breath comes out, but still no good. And then,
in a flash of insight, he finds the right verbal handle with
which to pick up Death Of Cow: Something absolutely
necessary to Cow—something without which Cow turns de-
cisively and permanently into Dead Cow, has gone out of
her. Since her breath has done just that, he decides to use
the word *breath* for it; but in order to prove he knows it
isn't really plain breath, he calls it Breath Of Life. Finally,
when he gets his Latin down pat, he fastens on the word
anima, or soul, to do the job. As bonus points, he gets the
words *animation, animate* and *animal,* and off he goes again.

You can take it from there: how he came to distinguish his own more loved and respected *rational soul* from the merely *sensitive soul* of the cow; how he invented the *vegetable soul* to explain the phenomenon of living, as opposed to dead, cabbage; and how, eventually, he started down the road to talking about all these souls—but especially about his own—as actually existing parts of the things they animated, as *reified* entities.

What must be carefully noted in all this is the fact that the further you wander from the original purpose of the distinction, the trickier the going gets. It is one thing to say that the soul has gone out of a living body and that, as a consequence, the body is now no longer a true body, but a corpse. It is quite another thing, however, to reify the departed ghost and then undertake to answer questions about its subsequent travels. You are on fairly safe ground in the first case: You are talking about an observed fact, death; and you are figuring it by the not inappropriate image of breath or soul. In the second case, however, you are talking, not about something empirically observed, but about the image you used to figure it; and you are attributing to the referent of that image a real existence which, in all honesty, you know very little about.

There is nothing necessarily wrong about that, of course. There may well be a real something, invisible and immaterial, which answers to the name Soul. But you don't know that. Perhaps you will say you do. Perhaps you think that God, in the Scriptures, assures us of it. Well, don't be so sure. Some biblical language certainly points in that direction. But on balance, more of the Bible's talk about human nature seems to dispense with the usage. The "immortality of the soul" is not a scriptural notion. When the Bible wants to get at the idea of man's eternal destiny outside the con-

fines of time, it has a strong preference for images like the
Resurrection of the Body and Everlasting Life.

Apparently, therefore, neither God nor man has given
any final assurance on the subject of the separate existence
of the soul. Certainly we should not despise the ancient and
widespread belief of the race that the soul survives the body's
death. But for the record, it ought to be noted that, in christian circles, this survivability was predicated only of the
human soul. Animal and vegetable souls were held to perish
when the matter they animated perished. Man's soul was
indeed said to persist; but the reasoning behind that conclusion was based chiefly on the theory that, unlike all other
souls, each individual human soul was directly created by
God and then infused into a body provided by cooperative
parents. That, however, is one of the most minimally scriptural notions of all. It derives mostly from highly spiritual
and otherworldly religions which set up an antagonistic
dualism between matter and spirit: The soul, as spiritual, is
good; the body, as matter, is evil. The goal of human life is
to get rid of the nasty old physical cocoon in which the
beautiful butterfly of the soul is imprisoned, so that, un-
fettered at last, it can assume its true nature and fly to God.

I am sure that many Christians—and all cheap-john-
funeral-parlor-poetry-writers—firmly believe that to be the
true Gospel. But it isn't. It is a thousand miles from the
judaeo-christian tradition. The beginning of the true teaching is that God made man—and precisely what we ordinarily mean by man: eyes, ears, nose, arms, buttocks, shin-
bones, ankles, toenails—God made all that, not just a
"soul," in his image. And the end of the true teaching is that
God redeemed man—flesh, bones, and all things appertain-
ing to the perfection of human nature—by the Resurrection
of the Body of Jesus. For a Christian, there are no Souls

(whatever that means) in heaven (whatever that means); there are only Risen Bodies (once again, whatever that means).

And there, at last, is one of the most important phrases in all theology: *whatever that means.* It should invariably be tacked onto every statement that even begins to predicate attributes of the Mystery: In the Godhead (whatever that means), there are three divine persons (whatever that means), subsisting (whatever that means) in one divine substance (whatever that means). For these are only our words—dim, groping, oysterish images which we point unsurely at something we cannot see and could not grasp if we did. We may indeed, as a result of our labors, come to some small understanding of what it is we are trying to say about the Mystery. And we may, perhaps, come to some slightly larger understanding of what it is we are trying to avoid saying. But even at our best, we remain light-years away from any understanding of what the Mystery, in itself, is really like.

As a matter of fact, the only words we can be precise about in the trinitarian example I just gave are the words *one* and *three.* And even there, I am a little tempted to add something like: "—if three is the right number, and if number is what God had in mind to tell us about." For after all, while we can be certain that three persons is the burden of Scripture and the teaching of the undivided church—so certain that we may rightly drum out of the corps anyone who says there are four—we have no knowledge of why God, in talking to us through Bible and church, picked the numbers he did. In all honesty, they don't make too much sense. It is quite possible that no one yet, in the entire history of Christianity, has stumbled over the real point of the information. But it doesn't matter. The purpose of orthodoxy is not

to tell you the whole truth, but to deliver intact to every suc-
ceeding generation the official boy scout set of images with
which to pursue the truth. Theology, therefore, is a hunt for
the Mystery—and the theologian is primarily a sportsman:
Even though he knows that as long as he lives he will never
get even one clear shot at the Beast, he is happy enough
keeping his guns oiled, and tramping through the woods.
Why shouldn't he be? At the end, the Beast has promised to
fall right at his feet.

Accordingly, the upshot of our investigation into the
original purpose of the soul/body distinction is this: "Soul"
was invented to pin down the distinguishing characteristic
of a *living* body; therefore, don't be too quick to come to
conclusions about its existence or nature when all you've
got for evidence is a *dead* body. The only evidence that gives
is evidence of absence. It's something. But it's not much.

Having said that, however, we may take up our lawful
freedom to go on at any length we like about the soul. It is
no small plaza in the city of our discourse, and we will only
impoverish ourselves if we make a vow never to pass an
afternoon in the park there. Just as long as the serious talk
about it is labeled as speculative—and the looser uses recognized as mere figures of speech—we can stay as long as
we like and, when we leave, know better than to lose the
wholeness of the Mystery in a blind alley.

Incidentally, speaking of "soul" as a figure of speech,
some priest friends and I once spent a late afternoon over a
bottle of vermouth. During the casual clerical chitchat, we
wandered into the subject of columbaria. The church, as
everybody knows, is on its financial uppers. Accordingly,
some of the more resourceful clergy have hit upon a neat
way to produce a little extra revenue: You set up burial

vaults for cremated remains in the basement of the church and sell the spaces to your parishioners. All it costs you is the price of marble, or whatever, to make the niches and their surroundings into a nice little chapel. Well, a few of the brethren got to talking about how much space you would need for each individual vault. The one priest there who had already built a columbarium said it took about 12″ x 14″, or something. In the space available in his undercroft, he claimed, that gave him room for some three hundred souls. I just couldn't resist. I said, "Souls! If that's all you're burying, you're missing out on a chance to make a million. For souls, all you need is a quarter-inch drill."

12

SUPERMAN

IF WE ARE GOING TO BE DEDICATED THEOLOG-ical sportsmen, however—if we're planning to do anything more than just shoot the breeze and knock back the Cinzanos—we had better get on with the job of selecting, cleaning and oiling the guns we need for the hunt. And when you put it that way, the most important rifle of all—the great elephant gun of an image—turns out to be the whole cluster of words and images which make up what we call the doctrine of the Incarnation: the teaching which says that Jesus of Nazareth is *true* God and *perfect* man in an *inseparable* but *unconfused* union in *one Person*—whatever all that means.

I shall, of course, attempt a few shots with it by and by. But first, one very fast but important reminder: I am not concerned with proving whether it's true or not. I happen to believe it is; you may, or may not, depending. All I want to do here is take a fresh look at it and see, first, whether we've got it straight, and second, whether we can use it to figure anything. As I said, the theologian's real work is not to prove that the Faith is true; only that it's interesting. Decisions about truth are, necessarily, the province of the faithful. Off we go then.

First, Jesus is God. More than that, he is true God. That means that even though we say it is the *second* Person of the Trinity who is incarnate in Jesus, we are using the word *true* to remind ourselves that since there is only one God, the Person who "came down from heaven and was incarnate by the Holy Ghost of the Virgin Mary" just has to be that same one God. He is all the God there is; there is no God at all that is not in him.

Confused? If you are, it may be because of the football-game image with which we sometimes try to figure the doctrine. As a figure, it's a bit thick in the flitch. It produces only fat-headed understandings of the Incarnation. Witness:

God the Father plays the first half of the game all by himself: The Son and the Holy Spirit sit on the sidelines from the dawn of creation right through to the end of the Old Testament. But then, in the fullness of time, the Father puts himself on the heavenly bench and sends in the Son for the third quarter. At the beginning of the last period, however, he decides he's got enough of a lead to risk using the rookies, so he pulls the Son and puts in the Holy Catholic Church to finish the game, now and then sending in the Spirit to kick field goals.

Put that baldly, of course, it sounds silly. But it, or something only a little less gross, is in many people's minds. And not without some justification. After all, that's the way it seems to have happened: The dispensation of Grace occurs historically, by degrees. And biblical phrases like "in the beginning" and "in the fullness of time" are extremely patient of "game" interpretation. Indeed, there is probably not a third-grade Sunday School teacher in the world who doesn't do it just that way. And since the church has a poor record of getting its members very far past the third grade, that's about the level of understanding of most of the membership.

But it won't wash. Scripture won't support it, and the Faith of the church won't touch it with a barge pole. The Word and the Spirit, as we said, are in on the act of creation, and Christ is in the Old Testament, and the Spirit of the Lord is in Isaiah, and Jesus *is* before Abraham was, and he had glory with the Father before the world existed. And as far as the church is concerned, whatever "three Persons in one God" means, it cannot mean three parts or three divisions, or three separable anythings. There is only *one* divine individual.

So if it's a game at all, it's got to be another ball game. One in which the whole team is in there all the way, working mysterious plays in which each takes turns carrying the ball, while one or both of the others block, run interference or just plain go invisible. And therefore, while it is indeed God the Son, the second Person of the Trinity, who becomes incarnate in Jesus, there isn't any of the Trinity outside him. The Father and the Spirit coinhere in everything he is and does. (It really isn't even correct to imagine his incarnation as a showing up, since he, as the one God he is, was always everywhere already.)

More on that later. Just note now how this *coinherence* of the Persons in each other and in one solves the problem which some people have with language like "he came *down* from heaven." They profess to be embarrassed by the implication that heaven is in the top story and that the Father had to send the Son downstairs to do his work. But no good theology has ever taken such language literally. It's an image—something with which to figure the mystery of God in Jesus. The fathers were perfectly clear that he never left heaven to get here. Witness the old Latin hymn:

> *Verbum supernum prodiens,*
> *Nec linquens patris dexteram . . .*

(The Word proceeding from above,/Yet leaving not the Father's side . . .). The spatial implication didn't worry them. They knew it was out of bounds.

As a matter of fact, this is as good a place as any to get in a general warning about the implications people go around discovering under every theological bed: Most of them turn out to be either false alarms or pussycats. If you know the Faith, and a couple of ground rules, they don't bother you at all. So panic not. You're dealing with a set of images, with plazas of meaning from which you can exit by many streets. Whatever *down* means, it can't mean downstairs. Maybe it means he came down from his first price. Or down off his high horse. Try it any way you like; just stay off the staircase.

For after all, *down* is no more, or less, difficult than the rest of the phrase. Why don't they fuss over *he*, for example? Obligingly enough, some people do. There is a pious backwater in the women's lib movement where you can find people who write services in which God is referred to as *she*. And of course, there is a corresponding angry swamp in the traditionalist movement where there is much weeping, gnashing of teeth and writing of letters to the editor about the outrage. Knuckleheads! Why don't they just remember not to leave the plaza *he* by way of the street marked *male*. Take *person* as the way out, and you're as safe as if you were in an armored car. *She,* on that basis, is obviously O.K. too. But by the same token, it's also totally unnecessary. It's no better and no worse than *he*. So if people with no theological horse sense want to lob rocks at each other, let them. Children must play. The rest of us should put away childish things.

All right. Jesus is true God, whatever that means. At the least, we've ticked off a few things it should not be allowed to mean under any circumstances. On to *perfect* Man.

It may be that there is no single word in Christian theology which has been more grievously misinterpreted than
the word "perfect" when applied to the humanity of Christ.
The original Greek which lies behind it is the word *telos:
an end accomplished,* the *completion* or *fulfillment* of anything. Accordingly, even though "complete" may sound a
little mild, I'm going to use it. "Perfect" has gotten so overblown that it needs to be taken down as many pegs as possible.

Therefore, when we say Jesus is perfectly human, we
mean he is completely human: His humanity is everyday,
common-garden humanity *in completion.* But see how alien
that is to the common view. "Perfect" is like "spiritual." It
sends people's minds straight out on extended ethereal trips.
The old dualism of evil matter/good spirit is so much a part
of us that, in spite of the promise of the resurrection of the
body, we can imagine human nature as perfected only if we
can somehow see it as abolished in favor of something
spiffier. We can figure Jesus as sinless only if we flesh him
out in something other than ordinary flesh.

When we imagine him as a child, for example, we somehow feel obliged to say that he was a little freak who never
hid when his mother called him, who always put his toys
away in his toy box, and who, when he got to the age at
which boys have wet dreams, piously refused to have any.
But that's theological folly. It's winning a minor battle at
the price of losing the whole war. The big things to be de-
fended about Christ are his Godhead and his Manhood. It
would be far better to bend the concept of his sinlessness a
bit than to lose sight of his humanity in the process of trying
to say how good it is.

Indeed, it might even be a good idea to come down a peg
from *completely* human just to make the point clear. Let's
call him *merely* human. Not, of course, in some disparaging,

proper sense of the word such as "merely stupid" or "mere boiled potatoes" but in the complimentary, slangy sense: "She was merely telling you the truth, Arthur," or "a mere five-carat diamond." Christ's perfect humanity, accordingly, is mere humanity: It's human, wholly human and nothing but human. (Jesus is God too, of course. But the first rule there is that, while you may never separate his two natures into two separate persons, you must not make a scrambled egg of him, either. He is not a blend of deity and manhood: His natures are inseparable but distinct. There is no manhood in his deity. And there is not one shred of God in his humanity, any more than there is in yours or mine—loose talk to the contrary notwithstanding. The union of the two natures is precisely a union, not an amalgamation.)

All this is necessary because almost nobody resists the temptation to jazz up the humanity of Christ. The true paradigm of the ordinary American view of Jesus is Superman: "Faster than a speeding bullet, more powerful than a locomotive, able to leap tall buildings in a single bound. It's Superman! Strange visitor from another planet, who came to earth with powers and abilities far beyond those of mortal men, and who, disguised as Clark Kent, mild-mannered reporter for a great metropolitan newspaper, fights a never-ending battle for truth, justice and the American Way." If that isn't popular christology, I'll eat my hat. Jesus—gentle, meek and mild, but with secret, souped-up, more-than-human insides—bumbles around for thirty-three years, nearly gets himself done in for good by the Kryptonite Kross, but at the last minute, struggles into the phone booth of the Empty Tomb, changes into his Easter suit and, with a single bound, leaps back up to the planet Heaven. It's got it all— including, just so you shouldn't miss the lesson, kiddies: *He never once touches Lois Lane.*

You think that's funny? Don't laugh. The human race is, was and probably always will be deeply unwilling to accept a human messiah. We don't want to be saved in our humanity; we want to be fished out of it. We crucified Jesus, not because he was God, but because he blasphemed: He claimed to be God and then failed to come up to our standards for assessing the claim. It's not that we weren't looking for the Messiah; it's just that he wasn't what we were looking for. Our kind of Messiah would come down from a cross. He would carry a folding phone booth in his back pocket. He wouldn't do a stupid thing like rising from the dead. He would do a smart thing like never dying.

If you don't believe me, look at the whole tradition of messiah figures in popular fiction. Superman is a classic but there are others just as good—and one that's even better— for illustrating our hunger for a nonhuman messiah. How about the sheriff in the typical "salvation" Western? Matt Dillon can be wounded but not killed, daunted but never defeated. He looks like a man, but he's really the avenging angel in drag. Just to prove it, the same old device is trotted out: You know Miss Kitty's business; and I know Miss Kitty's business; and it's a safe bet Miss Kitty knows her business. But Matt might as well be a Martian, for all the good it does him. The only belt he gets out of her comes in a little beer glass with a lot of talk.

Ditto the Lone Ranger, heigh-hoing around the days of yesteryear with Tonto, a white horse, no women, and a beltful of silver bullets, yet. Do you see? Everybody else is human; Doc, Festus, Quint, Kitty, the drovers, the sodbusters, the townsfolk, the bad guys. But the Messiah who saves them all is unbendingly, unflinchingly Divine.

Not convinced yet? That's because I haven't given you the clincher. These Western sheriffim are a little misleading.

They still, like Superman, have the appearance of humanity. It is not until we come to the ultimate popular messiah figure that we realize how much we despise our nature: We are so desperate to get rid of it that our imaginations will accept not only superhuman messiahs, but subhuman ones, too. Maybe you think I'm going to give you an essay on our longing to be saved by something classy like Technology, or Science, or The Computer. But I'm not. I'm still reading *TV Guide*:

❹ LASSIE—Drama

Lassie's problems: a snow goose and an ailing poodle. Part 2 of a four-part episode filmed at California's Vandenberg Air Force Base. Garth: Ron Hayes. Chaplain: Jack Ging.

A dog, for Christ's sake! Literally! Little Timmie goes schlepping all over the countryside getting himself lost, strayed or stolen, but he's practically the only human character in the show. Mother and Father are a couple of clowns who couldn't keep track of the movements of Mount Rushmore. And poor Jack Ging, having to play the Chaplain! Turn off the set. I can't stand to watch a grown man make a fool of himself. But no matter. Lassie *vincit omnia*. She will be beaten by bad men, bitten by alligators, clawed by mountain lions, and left for dead in the desert. But three days later! Home she comes with the snow goose on her back, the ailing poodle in an improvised litter, and in her mouth, Mother's wedding ring, Father's wallet and a note to pick up Timmie at the supermarket.

I hope I have convinced you that we can hardly be too fussy about keeping our view of the humanity of Christ completely, merely human. In any case, however, the last question to be dealt with is now in front of us: If Jesus is one-hundred percent man, how do you figure the union of his two natures in one Person?

Well, the old orthodox answer comes in the form of two rules of thumb. Rule 1: If you're talking about the *natures*, you give Jesus two of everything and you try your best not to mix them up. Rule 2: If you're talking about the *Person*, you can relax a little and let it sound as if you had forgotten Rule 1. (Rule 1 came out of the church's experience with the christological controversies of the fourth and fifth centuries—especially out of her response to some gentlemen named Apollinaris and Eutyches. Rule 2 arose in connection with a theologian by the name of Nestorius; it is called the *communication of idioms*. I don't know if that helps you, but I do have to flash my union card once in a while.)

Rule 1. Example: Jesus has two minds, one divine, one human.

QUESTION: Why do you have to say that?

ANSWER: Because if you don't, you welsh on what you've already said about his being true God and perfect man. Human thought and divine thought don't mix. Asking "Did Jesus think divine thoughts in his human mind?" shipwrecks you on the rock of incommensurability. It's apples and oranges—like asking, "What does E-flat smell like?" If you sneak divine thoughts into a human mind, you make it superhuman. That can be a lot of fun, of course, but it messes up the realities of salvation. He came to save *us*, in the barefaced human nature he gave us. But if the final product of his labors is a jazzed-up third something which is neither honest-to-God God nor honest-to-man man, then he didn't save *us*. He gave up on us and saved something else he liked better.

Get on top of it and look down. Suppose *you* were the highest thing in the universe, the cause of everything below you. And suppose that the frogs had eaten of the Lily Pad Of The Knowledge Of Good And Evil and messed themselves up royally. And suppose you decided to save them by becoming incarnate among them. How would you have to go about it? (Just for the sake of neatness, we should get the Latin formation straight: *Carn-* means flesh; *incarnation,* therefore, is enfleshment. Frog, in Latin, is *rana*; enfrogment should be *in + ran-* or *irranation.*)

In your irranation you must, above all else, take care not to foul up the frogginess of the frogs. After all, that's the very thing you're out to rescue from the detestable unfrogginesses they have committed. Accordingly, you will have to come down and dwell among them without intruding your nature into theirs in any way, shape or form. You, as you, must not be revealed among them, because that would violate the way *they* live. Your thoughts of political science, economics and chemistry must not be thought in their substance, because that's not their style. Your taste for fine wines, *escargots,* peperoni pizza, and bawdy songs must not once be indulged through the whole of your irranation; you will have to content yourself only with the best insects you can find, the jolliest croakings you can manage. Only that way could they rebuke you, as we rebuked Christ, for being "a Croaker and a Bugeater."

For if you were to violate any of those conditions, the Christfrog in whom you would be irranated would be just a freak; a frog whose mind, for example, had two compartments. The lower chamber would be merely froggy, but the upper one, gloriously human. And between them would be a trap door so that, even though your Christfrog would normally draw his thoughts only from the froggy part of his mind, he would always be able, in a pinch, to reach up through the trap door and get any human knowledge he might like or need.

But once again, that just won't wash. Go back to Jesus: If you posit a trap door through which his divine mind can leak heavenly secrets into his human mind—if you give his human intellect an inside track which no other human intelect has—then you simply make it nonhuman. And you come up with a lot of sillies. Like the human mind of Jesus in 20 A.D. knowing who shot John Kennedy. Which is just plain unreal. His *divine* mind knew, of course. But you don't ruin his humanity just for the sake of some easy synthesis you'd like to effect. The rule in theology is: When you've got two truths which you can't hold in harmony, you don't solve the problem by letting one of them go. You hang on tight and hold them both in paradox. At least that way you don't end up sweeping jewelry under the rug in the name of compulsive neatness.

"But," you say, "it's so hard to imagine what it would be like for Jesus to be both God and man."

Wrong. Once you know any theology at all, you make a distinction: If you're trying to imagine what it's like for God the Son, as he is in himself, it's not hard; it's impossible. So give up. But if you're trying to imagine what it was like for Jesus, in his humanity, it's a lead-pipe cinch. Just imagine that he felt just like you, because that's exactly what the doctrine says: He was perfectly, completely, merely *human*. And if you insist on looking for an answer to the question of how the divine works on the human in Christ, seek it in some way that doesn't, on the one hand, make a mishmash of them, or on the other, turn Jesus into some kind of committee of two locked in a thirty-three-year executive session. Perhaps the best way of figuring it is to say

that, in Jesus, the divine operates on the human in the order
of Grace and not in the order of nature. Which, of course, is
to say of Jesus's human nature exactly what we say of our
own—even when we talk about miracles.

Jesus didn't cast out demons by some superhuman power
nobody else had. He did it by the Grace of the Holy Spirit,
which everybody else has, and which lots of people have
used, if you believe the miracles of Scripture. And he didn't
get driven into the desert to fast and pray by some special
high-octane intellectual gas that leaked through the trap
door in his head. The Spirit drove him. Just as it drives us
—except we mostly get off the bus too soon. And when he
was little, his knowledge of Aramaic, and his knowledge of
the Scriptures, and his knowledge of carpentry all came in
the same way: humanly, not superhumanly. If he got any
heavenly help, it was the same help of the Holy Spirit you
and I get—which, in all honesty, is not too much when it
comes to memorizing verbs or learning how to use a draw-
knife.

"But," you say, "didn't Jesus know he was God?"

FIRST ANSWER: Yes. Because what else could he mean
by a phrase like "he that hath seen me hath seen the Father."

SECOND ANSWER: I don't know. He didn't say so in so
many words.

THIRD ANSWER: No, at least not for part of his life. When
he was a baby, he didn't even know he was a baby. How
could he know he was God?

FOURTH ANSWER: No. As a Jew, that formulation of his
mission was unavailable to him. He figured his identity in
other ways: Son of Man, Son of God, Son of David, Christ,
Lord, Brazen Serpent, Greater than Solomon, Bread from
Heaven. It even took the church a couple of hundred years
before it could say, "Jesus is God."

FIFTH ANSWER: You don't need an answer. It makes no difference whether he knew or not. He *was* God; and he *knew* how to save. Nothing more was necessary.

SIXTH ANSWER: It's a dumb question. Haven't you been listening to what I've been saying about the mere humanness of his human mind? Of necessity, he had to figure the answer to "Am I God?" with the human images he had at hand. Which he did. In the Gospels. The answers are all there; figure them out for yourself.

CORRECT ANSWER: Take your pick. I'm not in the question-answering business anyway.

I apologize for taking so long with my one example of Rule 1. I shall atone by giving two exceedingly brief examples of Rule 2.

The *communication of idioms* is theological shoptalk for the idea that, since the divine and the human in Christ are, in spite of all the difficulties, still to be taken as united in *one Person,* then you may attribute the idioms or properties of either nature to the one Person they both, in fact, are. As I said, you get some more relaxed usage this way: God died on the Cross. Well, obviously, God, as God, can't die. But if God is one Person with man in Jesus, then when Jesus dies in his human nature, the Person, the one Identity he is, may correctly be said to die too.

Again—to take the great original of this kind of talk: Mary is the Mother of God. Clearly, God, as God, neither needs nor has a mother. But it is a matter of record that when God decided to become man, he used a mother, just like everybody else. Therefore, since he is one Person with Jesus, and since Mary is the mother of Jesus, the correct answer to the question "What was the name of the Person who was born of Mary?" can be either "Jesus" or "God," as you like. The answer "God" made people like Nestorius nervous. It still does. I happen to like it; you may not. Fortunately, it's one of those matters of taste we don't have to fight about—unless you try to tell me I am bound by some metaphysical necessity to dislike it.

If you do that, I shall call you a Nestorian and throw empty wine jugs at you.

13
BOOKKEEPING

AM I MISTAKEN, OR DO I DETECT A NOTE OF annoyance? "Some nerve!" you mutter to yourself. "Where does he get off, threatening me? I feel like throwing a couple of bottles myself. Back in chapter nine he promised to begin talking about the Mystery. Here he is now at thirteen, and all he has given me is more talk about language and four chapters full of pronouncements on what the Mystery is not. People who live in glass houses . . ."

All right. Pax. Fins. King's X. Be a Nestorian if you like. This is the only way I know how to do it.

Because as far as our minds are concerned, the Mystery remains stubbornly, maddeningly mysterious. Not that we don't have an existential grip on it: We touch it all the time—and not just in religious ways. It isn't only by anointing the feet of Jesus while he was on earth, or by receiving the Sacrament of his Body and Blood that we grasp it. It is in us, with us and under us every moment of our being— and in, with and under everything else too. And not that *it* doesn't have a grip on *us:* It is precisely the hand of the Mystery that holds us so alarmingly and gloriously *outside nothing* and *in being.* It's just that when we try to talk about it, we inevitably find that we can be clearer about what it isn't than what it is. The best we can do is refine and sharpen the paradoxes by which we state it, reassess and reinterpret the images by which we figure it—go over our figures, if you like, and check them for false results.

At the end of the last chapter, I slipped into a usage which, while practically unavoidable, is particularly in need of reexamination. In talking about Mary as the Mother of God, I used the phrase "*when God decided* to become man.*" That, and the fundamental question it raises about the nature of the Mystery, are what this chapter is about.

On one level, saying "when God decided" is perfectly all right. It is anthropomorphism, just as every other usage is. To use it wisely, you simply have to bear in mind constantly that *deciding at a certain time* is not the best image of what God does. He doesn't sit around wondering, and then *one day* make up his mind. He just wills. And whatever he wills, he wills from all eternity. His mind is never anything but fully made up.

On another level, however, the phrase is bound to make trouble, because the "time" imagery is so strong that it keeps knocking at every door in the house until somebody lets it in. Perhaps you think that's all right—that as long as it doesn't track its time-mired feet in the front room, where God is, it can be let into the kitchen, where creation is. For after all, the world is temporal, and God acts in history, and revelation comes by degrees. Why can't you just put an unexpressed parenthesis in the phrase to clean it up? Why can't you say: "When (*from our point of view*) God decided"? Doesn't that succeed in keeping the mud out of the parlor?

No, because even with its feet thus parked on a mat, it's just biding its time. The minute you turn your back it will roam all over the place. Watch.

Jesus of Nazareth was born in the back of a stable near

Bethlehem in the year 4 B.C. (That's correct. Mercifully, though, it's not another paradox. It's the result of a mistake somebody made when the calendar was changed.) In any case, Christians believe that this same Jesus is the Word made flesh; he is God become man. Accordingly, it seems perfectly safe to hold that his birth is the beginning of a new departure in which God himself comes on stage in the Incarnation—that "when (from our point of view) God decided to become man," a new Mystery went into effect.

For most people, no doubt, that sounds cautious enough. It predicates time of God only in connection with something he did in time. He always willed to do it; but in this world, he did it on a certain day. But hold on. There is an implication there just itching to put its muddy feet all over your theology. If you don't watch it, you will quickly find yourself saying that, accordingly, this Mystery became operative only in 4 B.C., and only in Jesus.

Does that still sound all right? Watch some more. If this Mystery first went to work in 4 B.C., then it was unavailable to all the people who lived before that date. And if it is operative only in Jesus, then that means that Jews, Turks, or Infidels who died in 200 B.C., or Eskimos who died in 29 A.D., were never in touch with it. And that in turn means that the whole untimely lot of them are out of luck as far as getting hotel accommodations in the New Jerusalem is concerned. And that means they can all go to hell.

Notice how nicely we're progressing. We have now arrived at one of the more detestable enormities in the history of theology. And we have run smack into opposition with Jesus's own words: "I, if I be lifted up . . . will draw *all* men unto me."

Since most of the theologians who embraced this monster

were basically nice people, they had the grace to feel bad about not having room in the eternal Holiday Inn for so many people. So they proceeded to build, not with the hard cash of Scripture, but almost entirely on speculation, a couple of cheap motels along the Jerusalem road. These were run by Conrad Limbo, Inc. There was the *Limbus Patrum,* or Limbo of the Fathers, for all the ancient Greek worthies like Socrates; and there was the *Limbus Puerorum,* or Limbo of the Children, for all the little tykes who cashed in their chips before they had a chance to commit any sins.

Things are going swimmingly. We have reached the point of saying that God will give you cut-rate bliss on the outer marches of his favor, just for being a good egg. Which, of course, is exactly what Jesus did not say: "*I* am the way, the truth, and the life: no man cometh unto the Father, but by me." Morality, not forgiveness—Law, not Grace— has become the promise of your gospel. You are about to skid yourself into the world's all-time pile-up on the Jersey Turnpike of theology: A dump truck (Galatians) and a tractor trailer (Romans) owned by Paul & Co. are going to jump the divider and clobber you. Reformation Brothers' Towing will take a hundred years to unscramble the mess, and not even Twentieth Century Body and Fender will be able to get the dents out. All because you thought it was safe to take your eye off "when God decided . . ."

Let's go back, then, and make the run again. Only, this trip, not quite so recklessly:

"When (from our point of view) God decided to become man," he chose to be "incarnate by the Holy Ghost of the Virgin Mary." This time, we shall avoid the pothole of assuming that the birth of Jesus is the beginning of a new departure in the way God works in the world. Let us say instead that it was the culmination of a whole series of

transactions between God and Man—transactions by which
the one, unchanging Mystery works toward the building of
Jerusalem, the City of God.

That sounds better already. It fits nicely with the history
of the covenants, and it obviates the necessity of seeing
Jesus as the sole transaction in which the Mystery is at
work: On their own level, all the earlier transactions—
Adam, Noah, Abraham, Moses—were true steps in the
building of the City. The Incarnation is simply the supreme
transaction. The Death and Resurrection of Jesus are the
effective fulfillment of all that went before.

Accordingly, we may now view the proclamation of the
Gospel in a different light. In Jesus, God has made the
ultimate transaction, after which no other transaction will
ever be needed. God has, as it were, perfected a saving
product, and he now proceeds to distribute it. This is good,
too. It makes sense of the scandal of particularity we saw
in Abraham: God *particularizes* salvation, first in Israel and
finally in Jesus, precisely in order to *universalize* it. He
cuts out everybody, just so he can eventually draw in all.
He excludes, but only to catholicize.

We're holding the road pretty well. But how does the
result of the ultimate transaction become catholic? How
is the finally perfected product distributed to all? Well,
in the first instance, this is accomplished by a fellowship
of baptized people which is universal, for all men—by the
one, holy, catholic and apostolic Church, sent to proclaim
everywhere the Gospel of Jesus's full, perfect and sufficient
sacrifice, oblation and satisfaction once for all offered on
the cross.

How, though, shall we deal with the problem which, last
time around, eventually caused the crash? How do we get
the perfected product to those born too soon, or too far

away from the Holy Catholic Chain Store? Let us try it this way: Let us say that, while the church is the normal outlet for the fruits of the transaction, it is obvious that the distributing operation of Jesus is not limited to the church. This has the virtue of having some scriptural and creedal foundation: After his death on the cross, and before his resurrection, *he descends into hell,* into *the place of departed spirits.* He goes and preaches to *the spirits in prison.* He offers them an opportunity to accept the free gift he has just perfected in the ultimate transaction.

Good enough. That takes care of everybody who died before 29 A.D.—and without a single jerry-built limbo, at that. But what about the Eskimo in 29 A.D. who didn't even have an Eskimo's chance of getting preached to at all— who died in the frozen North while the church was still basking in the Mediterranean sunshine? What about all the poor souls who were too late for the early show and too early for the late one? Well, perhaps we can hold that the descent into hell was not meant to be taken as a single excursion, but as a perpetual visit. Maybe it should be taken to mean that Jesus is always there, continually offering his salvation to all who die without having heard it: If you don't get a chance to pick up your free gift at one of his franchised outlets during your lifetime, he will personally distribute his product door to door after death.

It's holding nicely. No limbos. Nobody left out. But what of the final question? What does it mean when we say that the *souls of the departed* will have a chance to accept or reject the free gift? The souls of the departed, if they exist in reality at all, are not human beings. A human being is soul and body; if you separate the two, you get a ghost and a corpse. Furthermore, in the tradition in which this usage of *soul* was most common, the soul after death was viewed as a poor, passive thing, incapable of doing or deciding anything. And worse yet, there is 2 Corinthians 5:10: "We must all appear before the judgment seat of Christ; that every one may receive the things done in his body, according to that he hath done, whether it be good or bad."

Oh, oh. Things are beginning to sound as if we've got a front wheel out of balance. The argument is up to speed, but it's developing a shimmy. Perhaps if we push it a little harder, we can cure it. Suppose we try saying that the descent into hell means, not a standing order by which Jesus offers the benefits of his saving transaction to the souls of the dead, but rather a willingness on his part to take some of the "deeds done in the body"—things done while people were still alive and, therefore, still people—as the equivalent of acceptance or rejection of the gift.

That only makes it worse. Apparently both front wheels are in bad shape. On the one hand, we are slipping from theology into bookkeeping: We are now obliged to work out a system for converting purely natural earthly deeds into acceptance of Christ. On the other hand, that turns out to be a tricky proposition. If we're not careful, we will steer ourselves right back into the same situation that caused the awful pile-up on the last trip: We are on the verge of saying once again that morality, not mercy, is the key to the City—that Law is, after all, the touchstone of Grace.

Of course, we might try to work up some way of saying that the "good deeds done in the body" are to be taken, not as good deeds which have power to earn salvation, but as evidence of a willingness to accept mercy. How about a system for converting the coin of morality into the scrip of forgiveness? Of course, that will involve a lot more bookkeeping. As a matter of fact, it will probably involve keeping two sets of books. . . .

Hey, listen. The shimmy is getting worse instead of better. I've got an idea. This heap we're driving has had it. Between the front end and the dents, it's going to nickel-and-dime us to death. Why don't we pull into the next dealership we come to and trade it for a new model?

14
TRANSACTING

AS I ANALYZE THE TROUBLES WE RAN INTO IN
the last chapter, it strikes me that they were caused—as
most theological calamities are—by unexamined assump-
tions. On the first trip out, we made the mistake of assuming that the Incarnation was a *new departure*. Inexorably,
that led us into a struggle to find a way of getting it to
tag up with all the people whose times or places were such
that they missed the boat. For if it really was something
new, then old human nature had to be viewed as totally cut
off from its benefits. From the birth of Jesus onward, we
had to see "natural man" as a disaster area fit only for con-
demnation, and "redeemed man in Christ" as the only locus
of the Mystery. Simple decency, of course, led us to posit
limbo in order to soften the obvious injustices of such a
view—and from there on, it was all downhill.

The second time around, we took the history of the covenants seriously and refused to see the Incarnation as a new
departure. But we went right on assuming that it was
fundamentally a kind of *transaction,* that the events by
which it was manifested—birth, teaching, miracles, cruci-
fixion, resurrection, ascension—were so many steps, the
sum of which comprised the totality of a rescue and salvage
operation. We did indeed manage to hold that this opera-

tion was in the works before Jesus: We caught on to the fact that the same Mystery is at work in all the covenants. But spreading the working of the Mystery over the length and breadth of history deals with only half the problem. The other half is the question of how the Mystery works. Is it completely contained, as it were, in the events of salvation history? Or would it be better to say that the saving events are contained in *it?* Are Jesus's death and resurrection, for example, the only communication of Atonement? Or is Atonement a vast Mystery of which Jesus's Death and Resurrection are just a single true, full, effective, preeminent communication?

Obviously, we opted for the former. We assumed that the Mystery was contained in the transactions by which we learned about it—that it could safely be spoken of as if it were operative only in the *pieces of business* presented to us in the revelation. And that, of course, led us straight back into the old problem of tagging up: How does a merely transactional Incarnation extend its effect to those who miss it? That, in turn, took us from theology to bookkeeping, and if we had kept on with it, we would soon have joined forces with the gentleman at the end of chapter ten who was holding himself up in the air at arm's length and trying to figure out how to change hands.

I suggest, therefore, that we take a much closer look at the connection between Mystery and transaction—that we reexamine the assumption that the operation of the Mystery can be equated with a series of *shticks* which God did at various times in the history of creation. My thesis is that transactional views of Christianity have caused more problems than we suspect, and that if we can manage to correct them, a lot of heretofore unresolvable conflicts may well just disappear. On with it then, beginning, as always, with a distinction.

The Mystery does indeed manifest itself through transactions; for this is, after all, a totally transactional world. Nothing happens here that isn't *done* somewhere, sometime, somehow, by somebody. If the Mystery wants to tip its hand among the likes of us, it's going to have to work up its shtick just like everything else. And it has. The covenants—from Adam to Jesus, from the Tree of Life to the Tree of Calvary—are all pieces of business. So there is no way of escaping transactional language when we talk about the Mystery—or transactional behavior on our part when we respond to it.

On the other hand, the Mystery is not only in the world, busy with piecework. It is also in God, totally busy just *being*. The Mystery as it is in God, however—before, during and after all worlds—isn't inching its way toward a goal it hasn't reached yet. In God, the end is fully present at the beginning; the beginning is fully realized in the end. God, in his mysterious relationship with the world, never changes his mind or his manners, never does anything he didn't have in mind before, never drops a stitch, pulls out a row, reverses engines or slams on the brakes. And therefore, while in one sense, everything he does in creation involves doing business with somebody, in another sense, he never does business with anybody. He doesn't trade. He doesn't transact. He doesn't haggle. He doesn't even really *do;* he just *"be's."*

That sounds strange until you look at the Gospels. Then, suddenly, it sounds right: Salvation as a gift given, not a bargain struck. A father who does not trade forgiveness for good behavior, but who kisses the prodigal son before he gets his confession out of his mouth. A vineyard owner who pays what he pleases, not what the laborers earn. A shepherd who allows no sensible business considerations to keep him from leaving ninety-nine sheep in jeopardy to bring one to safety. A wheat grower who runs his farm, not for profit, but for the sake of letting everything grow as it pleases till the end. An Incarnate Word who won't talk to Pilate; a Carpenter of Nazareth who saves the world by nailing down his own hands; a Risen Lord who runs everything by going away. A God, in other words, who does all things well by doing practically nothing right, whose wisdom is foolishness, whose strength is weakness—who runs this whole operation by being no operator at all and who makes no deals because, in the high Mystery of his being, he's got it made already.

There is, perhaps, no topic in theology on which more barbaric, fatuous, dumfounding things have been written than on predestination. I am not about to add to the confusion here, but I do want to insist that, in spite of its wretched history, the subject must be kept in the hopper for discussion. At the very least, it keeps before our minds this incomprehensible intractability of God. Much more than that, of course, needs to be said about it—and a good deal of it will have to be in paradoxical opposition to anything that predestination could possibly mean. But the impossible doctrine itself must never be skipped over. It is theology's star witness to the non-transactional nature of the Mystery at its deepest level—to the truth that even though creation may be mightily out of hand, he's got it all together from the beginning, without moving a solitary muscle or trading a single horse.

But enough. That's another hunt, and another beast. Time now to draw a bead on the Mystery through our newly purchased one-hundred-power non-transactional sight. Aim high and bring the gun down slowly on the subject.

Consider first how the act of creation is not a transaction, even though we ordinarily imagine it to be one. When we think of God as the cause of the world, we almost invariably figure the Mystery involved by forming a sentence whose main verb is in the plain, unvarnished past tense. We speak of his creating as if it were a piece of business he once did: Last summer, I *made* a boat, *closed* on a house, *played* a gig. In the beginning, God *created* the heaven and the earth.

But that isn't really the case. It is a usage which conceives of the act of creating as an act of *starting up*—which seems to say that all you need God for is to get things going, and that once he has created, the world needs no more causing. He could, of course, destroy it, but short of that, it continues to be on its own steam.

As St. Thomas pointed out, however, that's not so. If God wanted to destroy the world, he wouldn't have to do anything; he would have to stop doing something. God is not only the initial cause of the world at its beginning; he is the present and immediate cause of the world at every moment of its being. Things exist, not because he made them, but because he makes them, everywhere and everywhen: Of course he made them at the beginning; but that's only one moment in the billions of instants of time to which the Mystery of his creative act is eternally contemporary.

Examine next, therefore, what that means as far as his relationship to the world is concerned. It is not as if he once made the world and then turned it loose. That is a view which allows you to see history as something the world did largely apart from God. And it allows you to see his repair and rehabilitation of history as a superadded trans-action—a new *shtick* by which he gets back into a show from which he was mostly absent after the opening number.

Once again though, that can't be right. God creates everything at every moment. The freedom of the world to wander at will is a freedom it has, not after it gets loose from God, but while it is locked forever in the viselike grip of his creative power. That means that all its sins, all its enormities, all its bloodshed, all its savagery, occur right in the palm of his hand because his hand is what *lets it be*. (The phrase, you will note, is pregnant. In its prim and proper sense, it refers to his actively creative power: *Let there be!* "Light! Firmament! Sun! Moon! Stars!" But the divine Wisdom also makes a fool of himself with creation. He leaves it free. Within the aggressive *Let it be!* he includes a slangy, laissez-faire *Leave it be*. "Whales? Birds? Cattle? Men? *Leave 'em be*. Anything they want is O.K. by me." The Infinite Card Sharp, the master of every deal, is also just the Infinite Kibitzer, hanging around doing nothing. The Ultimate Agent is also the Ultimate Patient.)

But notice what kind of world that produces. The ordinariness we see around us and take for granted turns out to be an illusion; and the strangeness, the fingerprints of the Mystery, turn out to be the reality.

There are three possible views of the world, each of which is true. The first is that the world consists entirely of winners: Every single thing that is, is a triumph of being, shouting from the housetops its praise of the Mystery by which it stands *extra nihil* and *extra causas*. The second view is that the world, at any given moment, consists of fifty percent winners and fifty percent losers: The river is wearing down the rock; the weasel is doing in the goose; these shoes are killing me. The last view is that the world is all losers: The shoes go to dust, the dust goes down the river, the river is evaporated by the sun and the sun itself goes cold. The last course at the banquet of creation is frozen entropy—with no chocolate sauce.

On any given day, of course, you and I will be in such a mood as is appropriate to one or the other of these *Weltanschauungen: Exultant,* as we and the surf frolic together. *Game,* as we take up arms against slings and arrows. Or stone-cold *sad,* when we sit by the waters of Babylon and the songs of Zion stick in our throats.

But on every given day, with every given thing—and on all the ungiven, unending days of eternity—*God is in all three moods at once.* Do you see what that means? He is always winning, always struggling and always losing. He doesn't win and lose by turns, in transactions. He doesn't simply win on Sunday, simply struggle on Thursday, simply die on Friday, and simply rise again on Sunday. He does all three on all days. He loses on the first Sabbath, because creation is free to defeat him at the Tree. And he reigns from the Tree on Good Friday, because in the Mystery of predestination, it is precisely by losing that he wins.

Therefore, the transactions by which he seems now to win, now to lose, are not, at their deepest root in him, transactions at all. They are rather revelations by degrees of what the Mystery is all at once. They are not bits of business which God transacts in order to get somewhere. They are sacramentalizations, outcroppings—effective and real manifestations under the form of transactions—of the one, constant, non-transactional Mystery by which he sets the world as a seal upon his heart, and forevermore has no place else to go.

The supreme outcropping of the Mystery, of course, is Jesus. But what happened in and through Jesus was not something new that God finally got around to plugging into the system. Rather it is what God was really up to all along, finally and effectively sacramentalized. In Jesus, we see thrust up before our eyes what has always worked below the surface of the world. Looking at history without Jesus in it is like looking at the Great Plains and trying to figure what the earth is made of: You never really catch on to the fact that, except for the surface, it's mostly stone. But when you come to the Rockies, you understand: There before you is a clear outcropping of what lies beneath the plains.

So with Jesus. Leave him out of the world's history, and people will simply spend their days being glad when they can and sad when they must. They will try to win until they finally lose, and then they will curse God and die. But put his Death and Resurrection into the picture, and suddenly all the winning and all the losing are revealed as God's chosen métier.

Follow that to the end and see how it eliminates once and for all the problem of tagging up with those who somehow miss the Incarnation. We call Christ's dying and rising the Paschal Mystery, the Passover Mystery. But seen in the light of a non-transactional view, this isn't just typology anymore. It's a flat assertion that the Passover and the Resurrection are, beneath the surface, *the same thing*. You don't have to work up some system for getting the Israelites in the wilderness in touch with Christ: They already were, long before Jesus turned up on the scene. And so were Adam, Noah, Abraham, Isaac and Jacob. And so, to take it all the way, is everybody and everything that is.

Christ wins in every triumph and loses in every loss. Christ dies when a chicken dies, and rises when an egg hatches. He lies slain in the wreckage of all Aprils. He weeps in the ruins of all springs. This strange, savage, gorgeous world is the way it is because, incomprehensibly, that is his style. The Gospel of the Incarnation is preached, not so that we can tell men that the world now means something it didn't mean before, but so that they may finally learn what it has been about all along. We proclaim Christ crucified, the formless, uncomely Root Out Of A Dry Ground, in order to show men, at the undesired roots of their own being, the Incarnate Word who is already there, making Jerusalem to flourish. We do not bring Jesus to people or people to Jesus. We preach the Word who sends their roots rain, whether they hear or whether they forbear.

And so at last, the theological Rube Goldberg contraptions go into the trash can. At Auschwitz and Buchenwald, the Jews died in Christ and Christ in them. No limbos. No bookkeeping. If the church never got around to them—or if it did, but put them off with rotten manners—Christ still draws all men to himself. He descends into every hell. The Incarnate Word preaches on all days, to all spirits, in all prisons. The Good Shepherd has other sheep, and he flatly refuses to lose a single one.

15
REDUCING

WE WOULD BE DOING ONLY HALF THE JOB, however, if we were to stop our anti-transactional crusade at this point. To be sure, it helps greatly to see Jesus as the supreme outcropping—the grand Sacrament—of the Mystery of the Word's relationship to the world. It sorts things out. It reminds us that when we deal with mystery, we have to do justice to two things at once: the non-transactional Mystery itself; and the transactional plausibilities, the earthly signs, by which the Mystery makes itself known to us.

But Jesus is not the only sacrament. Once the process of sacramentalizing the work of the Word reaches the intensity it does in Jesus, it precipitates a whole shower of further sacraments: first, the *church,* which is the sacrament of Jesus; then the *sacraments* properly so called by which the church celebrates the Mystery of Jesus. And if it was difficult to keep sign and Mystery in balance when we talked about Jesus, it will be even more difficult when we talk about the church: Transactional views make mischief all along the line. The further down you go, the more trouble they make.

In Jesus, the union between the Mystery and its sign is unique. The Mystery, to put it still another way, is the im-

117

mortal and invisible Wisdom of God, mightily and sweetly ordering all things into the City; it is the eternal Word, bringing creation as a bride to his Father's house. The sign is the humanity of Jesus, his very flesh and blood—the mere one hundred sixty pounds or so of meat and bone in which dwelt all the fullness of the Godhead bodily. But the union between those two natures is a union in one Person —in the Person of the Word.

It is not terribly important to know precisely what that means. The crucial thing to know is that it is meant to point to a uniqueness, to a situation in which, while we must be careful to do full justice to each nature (Rule 1—remember?), we may also predicate the properties of either nature of the Person (Rule 2, the communication of idioms). Admittedly, there is the ever-present danger of either watering down his Deity so that he is no longer God, or gussying up his humanity till he turns into Superman; but that danger is kept under some control by the fact that both are inseparably, unconfusedly one in him. When you pick up either of them with any deftness at all, you always say something appropriate about him. You may carry on for six weeks about nothing but his Godhead, or for a year and a half about his manhood alone: Just as long as you don't say anything that violates the subject you happen to be on, you hit the bull's-eye on the subject of him every time.

This safety feature—this net so reassuringly rigged under the theological high wire—disappears when you come to speak of the derivative sacramentalizations of the Mystery. The Church, Baptism, the Eucharist, the Priesthood—all these should probably be spoken of with a little reserve. Jesus, on the one hand, may be seen as the great Sacrament of the Mystery—the Mystery itself supremely and personally present in the flesh. The Church, on the other hand,

while it may be seen as just as real a presence, should not
be viewed as so eminent a one. The church is a sacrament
once removed, as it were: Jesus is the effective Sign of the
Incarnation; the church is the sacrament of that Sign.

In the long run, it's all the same, existentially. The
church, for example, really is Jesus in his members: "He
that receiveth you receiveth me." The Eucharist is nothing
less than the fullness of Christ: "This *is* my body; this *is* my
blood." But intellectually—that is, in the only way we can
pick these things up theologically—it's not the same at all.
There is no union in one Person to catch you if you slip.
Whatever *Jesus* says, the Word says, because they are one.
That may give you some problems of interpretation, but
they're not bad. However, it is simply not true that whatever the *church* says, Jesus says. And it is definitely not
true that Jesus can safely be said to do whatever the church
does. Mother Church has said and done some of the damn-
dest things. She has at times been heavily into the cooking
sherry. There have been centuries which found her pretty
much confined to her room with the vapors.

When we come to speak of the church and the sacraments, therefore, the danger of overstatement or misstate-
ment is with us in spades. First, we have to be more careful than ever to avoid reducing the Mystery of Jesus to
some two-bit plausibility. Second, we have to resist far more
strenuously the temptation to gussy up the sign and turn
it into a substitute for the Mystery. And finally, we have
to be supremely judicious about transactions: Everything
the church does is just a piece of business; but it is done as
a communication of the Word, who, in his heart of hearts,
is no businessman at all. Clearly, the possibilities for confusion, tomfoolery, fakery and mischief are practically un-
limited.

Take first the temptation to reduce the Mystery to a plausibility. It has been succumbed to so often, and for so long, that many Christians, and perhaps most non-Christians, actually believe the plausibilities to be the true Gospel. Consider for example, the idea that the church is in the world to teach men the difference between right and wrong.

The president of the Rotary Club leans toward the clergyman on his right and makes small talk to kill time until the hour of the parson's speech: "Well, Reverend, it's good to have you here. We need to hear from you people every now and then. There's just no moral values anymore. I'll bet if some of these kids with long hair went to church and heard what you fellows have to say, they wouldn't be messing around with sex and pot, eh?"

The good father, of course, quickly tucks a heaping spoonful of rice pudding into his mouth and mumbles something like, "Mmmh?!" His first thought, however, is probably more like, "!@*#*&!@*#!!" And his second thoughts, while more printable, are even less tolerant:

"a. This guy hasn't darkened a church door all year. And it probably wouldn't help if he did. As far as he's concerned, the Gospel equals the Ten Commandments, and the Church is society's moral cop on the beat. That's all he's prepared to hear.

"b. If I hear one more crack about long hair, I'll scream.

"c. If I get one more knowing wink about teen-age sex, I'm going to get every member of the Ministerial Association to promise to copulate in public at least once a week.

"d. Really though, it's probably just as well neither he nor the kids go to church: Besides their being totally unprepared to hear that the Gospel is about Mystery and not

morals, the church is almost as unprepared to say it. God
help us all if we ever get religion.

"e. Now I have to get up and be polite to this monster
of a misunderstanding. I think I'll tell proctologist jokes
instead.

"f. I hate myself."

Morality, however, is only one of the plausibilities to
which the Mystery is regularly reduced. It is just as likely
that our short-suffering priest, had he been thrown to the
tender mercies of the program chairman on his right, would
have been regaled with an equation of the Gospel and
philosophy: "We certainly need more religion, Father. If
people only had faith, they wouldn't be so confused about
the meaning of life. It's lack of faith that gives people
ulcers."

And while the reverend gentleman was gagging on his
rice pudding, he would, this time, have run the following
mental course:

"Bleech! People like him should be strapped in a chair
and have the entire Book of Job read to them very slowly
in Hebrew, Greek, Latin and English. The meaning of life,
indeed! How many uncomprehending deathbeds has he
hung around? How many total losses has he spent hours
counseling? How many irretrievable misunderstandings has
he had to admit he had no answers for? Phony baloney.
And that bit about no ulcers. Hasn't he ever looked at a
crucifix? Faith can punch as many holes in you as anything. As a matter of fact, given this mess of a world, anybody without holes in his gut should probably be written
off as an insensitive clod, guilty of serenity in the first degree. As if the Gospel ever excused you from getting your
tail kicked in: 'The disciple is several comfortable cuts

above his master, alive and well in cloud-cuckoo-land.'
Gack!"

Finally, however, had our dominie landed next to someone more honest and less earnest, he would undoubtedly
have had it made clear to him that his luncheon companion
"never was, to be honest with you, Father, very much when
it came to religion."

But this would not displease the true shepherd of the
flock as much as might be expected. "At last," the pastor
would muse to himself, "one ray of hope. I get so sick of
listening to malarkey. If this guy only knew it, he's ready
for the Gospel. Religion is a necessary evil. It's the unavoidable transactional slop you have to wade through in order
to lay hold of the Mystery for yourself. But in Christianity,
religious acts are not transactions in their own right. They
don't get you into heaven or keep you out of hell. They
don't earn you a nice wife, or good kids, or two weeks in
Aruba, or the combination to the superfecta at Aqueduct.
They just deliver you to the Mystery. Which is like being
delivered to the lady or the tiger: It could be great or it
could be terrible; and in either case, it might be both. But
it is at least an adventure, and not some dumb transaction
by which the Great Bookkeeper In The Sky can be per-
suaded to fudge figures for you.

"If only they could see that Christianity starts by telling
you that you have no place left to go because you're already
home free; and no favor to earn because God sees you in
his beloved Son and thinks you're the greatest thing since
sliced bread. All you have to do is explore the crazy Mystery of your acceptance. Why do they always want to do it
the hard way?"

Let's leave the padre there. He's on the right track. The
church's temptation to welsh on the Mystery, to fake it, to

reduce it to a plausibility, to equate it with morality, philosophy or religion, must be fought to the death. For there is no escaping the consequences. She may think she is meeting the world on a basis it is prepared to accept, but she's wrong. What the world is prepared for on these subjects is mostly to hate them—and to hate anybody who peddles them as well. The children of this world are wiser in their generation than the children of light. They know that morals, philosophy and religion are not catholic tastes: They are the province of ideologues, scoundrels, interest groups, specialized talents, sincere people and other fanatics.

But what the world in its wisdom does not know is that its only protection against these unwelcome sectarian plausibilities is the even more unwelcome foolishness of the Mystery. For that alone is catholic. That alone goes to the root of every man's being. That alone, like spinach, is good for him, even if he doesn't like it. That alone is capable of nourishing the great unwashed generality of creation: the slob and dilettante, the genius and the moron, the owl, the pussycat, and the beautiful pea-green boat.

If it is objected that Mystery is a dumb answer to the world's questions, the objection is sustained. On two grounds: Yes, it's a dumb answer, because all the world ever does is ask dumb questions—like, How can it get home? when it's already there; and, How can it find favor? when it's already got it. And yes, it's a dumb answer, because it's literally *dumb:* sheep-before-her-shearers, silent-before-Pilate, still-as-the-grave, plain, unanswering, speechless, ask-me-no-questions-and-I'll-give-you-no-pious-pap, *dumb.*

But it is the answer!

16
FAKING

I KNOW. THAT'S ASSERTION, NOT PROOF. BUT listen, by this time, we're either friends or enemies. So, Three Cheers, or Tough Luck, as the case may be. On to the temptations to fake the sign.

The gist of them all is that they resolve the tension between the non-transactional Mystery and the transactional sign by making the sign so spiffy that, for all practical purposes, it does duty for the Mystery. It's the old Superman temptation applied to the church and her institutions.

Simple illustration first: Jesus instituted the Sacrament of his Body and Blood by commanding his disciples to eat bread and drink wine in remembrance of him. Human nature being what it is, however, it wasn't long before somebody got the idea that the bread for the Sacrament ought to be something special. It wasn't enough, apparently, that by Jesus's own words, any old bread would be nothing less than his true, risen and glorious body really present in a high mystery. They had to have Superbread. And so, in accordance with Murphy's Law (if a mistake can be made, it will be), the angelic fish-food communion wafers were invented: snow white, unleavened, crumbless, odorless and tasteless. And made by nuns. Out of rice flour. Without salt. In little waffle irons. With holy monograms on them.

125

And lest it be thought that this bent for spiritualizing the sign is just a bit of popery-jiggery, consider the protestant Communion Service. Store bread is used, but the temptation to cut off the crusts is more than the elders can stand. So there sit the elements: piles of white cubes, totally bereft of the touch of fire that brought them into being; and trays with shot glasses full of grape juice so that the church can go Jesus not one, but two, better. She improves on his manners by being more sanitary, and on his morals by not using wine. Fearful and wonderful!

But not, in the long run worth much more than a laugh. It's the purifying of other signs that makes more trouble. Take the Priesthood, for example.

The sign of the Ministry of the church is, quite clearly, the group of people designated as ministers. This designation takes place, for openers, at a service called ordination; but the important thing about it is that it continues. The Ministry is recognized in the church by function: The minister is the fellow up there doing the bread-and-wine thing or the baptizing-with-water thing, or the forgiveness thing, or the preaching thing. To do all those things, Jesus initially selected a ragtag lot of fishermen, tax collectors, peasants and intellectuals. He told them that when they broke bread, he would be really present; that whenever they forgave anybody, he would stand by their decision; and that when they preached his word, they would move mountains.

Once again, though, it wasn't enough. By and by, the idea got around that just plain people wouldn't do for so holy a sign. They had to have Superpeople. So they started down the road to the present ruin of the Ministry. They did manage to avoid one pothole: Except for a few fanatics called Donatists, the church never said that the unworthiness of ministers hindered the sacramental working of the

Mystery. She kept, as her official position, the sensible view that a mass said by a priest with his hand in the till, or a baptism performed by a minister who didn't believe in anything, was still valid.

But that was about it. For the rest, she went gleefully about the old business of going Jesus five, six or a baker's dozen better. Priests had to be nifty people: At various times in her history she has, for various reasons, insisted that they be single people (because marriage is O.K., you understand, but not that O.K.); male people (because women are swell, sure, but all that menstrual business is decidedly unpleasant); people without crime or impediment (because, of course, the church is composed entirely of forgiven sinners, but you have to draw the line somewhere to keep the riffraff out); and they also had to be smart people, good people, balanced people, charming people, diplomatic people, talented people, people who never got drunk, never swore, never told salty stories, never had mad loves, and who, in addition to all that, would be willing to work for next to no money at the job they did, even though they were not allowed to make a buck at anything else. There was even a time when lacking the *canonical digits* was an impediment to ordination: If some poor soul had lost a thumb or forefinger, he was considered unfit matter for the sacrament.

The result of all these nifty qualifications was twofold. First, it produced the poor, freaky, whacked-up thing that for centuries has passed for the ministerial sign of the Mystery of Christ. A list like that attracts a lot of nuts, rascals and three-dollar bills. And when it does attract even moderately normal people, it drives half of them out of their heads when they try to fulfill all its contradictory requirements. And it drives half of the other half out of the ministry when they think they haven't fulfilled them. And half of the last quarter into smugness when they think they have. The remaining eighth—the group who know they have fufilled them, and who also know the precise degree to which everybody else has not—become bishops, thus winning the game.

Second, however, the Superpeople list results in a situation in which not even bishops win. The sign becomes so important that the Mystery is lost in the shuffle. Since the church seems so insistent on all these *requisita* and *desiderata,* the world obligingly takes her at her word and judges her accordingly. She has advertised the omnicompetence, wisdom and general niceness of her priests; when the world finds (as it always does) that the product is not as advertised, it complains loudly and boycotts the store. And it serves her right. She advertised the wrong product. She was in the Mystery business, but she took the easy way out and peddled plausibilities instead.

Once again, however, the damage done by this particular puffing up of the sign of the Mystery pales before the next example. A strung-out ministry and an anticlerical world are nothing compared to the results of the aggrandizement of the church herself as an institution.

First of all, what is she, really? Well, she is the Body of Christ—an earthly society which, somehow, is Jesus himself in his members. She is not a club of Jesus enthusiasts, or a sectarian fellowship of like-minded pals. She is a great, gangling hulk of a girl, a huge, catholic net dragged indiscriminately through the world. Her admissions' procedure guarantees that she will never be otherwise: She pours water over little babies about whose opinions and temperaments she knows absolutely nothing, and blithely pronounces them full-fledged members.

From such a coarse screening process, no one in his right mind should ever expect more than chronic diversity, punc-

tuated, with luck, by an occasional agreement or two. And
yet. Murphy's Law. We did it again. We faked her natural
multiplicity into a monolithic unity. We pretended that an
institution composed entirely of sinners could somehow, as
an institution, be pure. We talked ourselves into believing
that a crowd of people who by necessity would hardly ever
agree even about easy things would infallibly get all the
hard things right. We made believe that the Holy Spirit
would use a totally political entity without ever letting poli-
tics into the act. We turned an absurd, Gospel-proclaiming
gaggle of geese into an efficient question-answering machine. And we fobbed off on ourselves—we who, like the
rest of the race, can barely organize our way out of a wet
paper bag—the solemn proposition that, because we were
the church, we had access to some divine managerial com-
petence that the world could never have.

What we forgot is that while the sign is always the sign
of the Mystery, it also continues to be, in an important
sense, nothing more than itself: It remains heir to all its
natural ills as well as all its natural glories. The bread of
communion can indeed be delicious, fragrant and warm
from the oven; but it can also go moldy. So can priests. And
so can the church: Her political processes can be as good,
or as corrupt, as any institution's. Her answers to questions
may prove as wise as can be, or as goofy as all get-out. As
the sign that she is, she is not necessarily better or worse than
the U.S. Senate, the American Bar Association or the PTA.
Except that, on the principle that what is good is difficult
and what is difficult is rare, goodness in the institutional
church—like goodness in violinists, cooks and street sweep-
ers—is bound to run a poor second to the sheer volume of
mediocrity, ineptitude and downright venality.

A couple of illustrations, therefore, of the fakery.

Take the idea of infallibility. Obviously, there is a legiti-

mate sense in which we must say the church is infallible:
She must have an infallible grip on the Gospel. If after two
thousand years, we are not perfectly certain we are supposed to be preaching that Jesus died and rose again, then
we had best file for bankruptcy. But knowing for sure what
the Gospel is, is a very modest business. All you need is the
Bible and the creeds—which is precisely the slim but ade-
quate area of agreement that most Christians have reached.

It is the step from that infallibility to a larger one that
brings us to grief. It is one thing to claim that the infallible
answer to "How long was Jesus in the tomb?" is "Three
days." It is quite another to suppose that we have infallible
answers to any and all questions which we or the world
might choose to ask.

To do the church credit, she has so hedged about the
doctrine of papal infallibility that it requires, as Chesterton
pointed out, less of an act of faith than taking your family
doctor's word that his prescription won't hurt you. Infallibility has been restricted to the Pope only, speaking ex
cathedra only, and on faith and morals only. And as if that
weren't cagey enough, all those conditions are open to interpretation to one degree or another.

But still, the hedge isn't tight enough. Point one: Why
should the church be expected to have any infallible *machinery*? In a free world, God reveals himself without getting pushy. He does not override the nature of the earthly
agents he uses; he works through them. He inspired the
Epistle to the Galatians, not by putting the author in a
trance and speaking through his lips, but by taking a very
angry Paul and letting him rip. He gets the supernatural
across by mysteriously allowing nature to do what comes
naturally.

Now the church is a crowd of people. Its nature will be

to operate like any other crowd of people: In its corporate judgments it will make mistakes. As a matter of fact, if we take history seriously, it will probably get more things wrong than right. Only the test of time will tell which was which. Why then, given that nature, should it be expected that somewhere in its fabric there will be a button which you can push to get infallible answers to your questions?

That's a poser. It was undoubtedly because of its manifest absurdity that a severe limitation was imposed on the types of questions for which infallible answers would be available: Only Faith and Morals would get red-carpet treatment. But that's no less absurd. And it's a giveaway besides. First of all, questions of faith and morals have always been among the most hotly debated of all. Disagreements about them have been rampant and endemic, and agreements have displayed a tendency to be short-lived. To be sure, if you want to set up an administrative procedure by which a pope or a council can rule, supreme-court style, that x, y or z is the church's official teaching and that gainsayers must henceforth shape up or ship out, all right. But if you go beyond that and claim that some basically political process of argument and pronouncement will automatically produce the Right Ruling, you're off base. Political bodies don't work that way; when they pretend they do, watch out. And it makes no difference what body or institution you select as your infallibility button. People have at times tried to claim that an ecumenical council, if you could manage to call one, would be infallible. But that's no better than the Papacy. And, when you think about it, the Papacy is no less political than that.

But second, the restriction of infallibility to questions of faith and morals is a giveaway because of the inclusion of morals. It betrays a fatal tendency to confuse apples and oranges, Mystery and plausibility. If they would limit it to faith alone, maybe I would trust them. But when they tack on morals, I lose all confidence in their judgment. What's so all-fired important about morals? Why isn't it just as important for us to have infallible answers about Economics? Or Art? Or Child Rearing? Or Cooking, for that matter? God knows, the number of evil cooks in the world is enough to make any reasonable man long for guidance from on high.

I'll tell you why morals got up there in the Top Two. It's because they thought it was the church's real business. But it wasn't, and it isn't, and it must never be allowed to become so. The church is not in the morals business. The world is in the morals business, quite rightfully; and it has done a fine job of it, all things considered. The history of the world's moral codes is a monument to the labors of many philosophers, and it is a monument of striking unity and beauty. As C. S. Lewis said, anyone who thinks the moral codes of mankind are all different should be locked up in a library and be made to read three days' worth of them. He would be bored silly by the sheer sameness.

What the world cannot get right, however, is the forgiveness business—and that, of course, is the church's real job. She is in the world to deal with the Sin which the world can't turn off or escape from. She is not in the business of telling the world what's right and wrong so that it can do good and avoid evil. She is in the business of offering, to a world which knows all about that tiresome subject, forgiveness for its chronic unwillingness to take its own advice. But the minute she even hints that morals, and not forgiveness, is the name of her game, she instantly corrupts the Gospel and runs headlong into blatant nonsense.

The church becomes, not Ms. Forgiven Sinner, but Ms. Right. Christianity becomes the good guys in here versus the bad guys out there. Which, of course, is pure tripe. The church is nothing but the world under the sign of baptism. It is the mixture as before, dampened. It contains as many scoundrels as any other sampling—and they practice their scoundrelism with as much vigor as the best of them. The rewards of divination, of course, are smaller nowadays than they used to be. But there was a time when the church could have bought and sold the Oval Office.

So hand me no infallible machinery. I can't believe it, and I won't trust it. It not only fobs off on me a transaction when it should be giving me a Mystery. It even gives me the wrong transaction. But lest all this be taken as anti-romanism, behold the protestant parallels:

Parallel one: The Bible *only* is infallible.

Nonsense. The Bible is indeed God's Word Written, and it most infallibly contains all things necessary for salvation. But it is also a thing. It is not the Mystery; it is just another sign of it. And as the sign that it is, it obeys the law of its nature: It's a book. It came into being like a book: bit by bit. It lives like a book: in the mind of its readership. And it would die like a book, if it had no readers. How foolish, then, to think that the Bible alone can ever be anything. How idle to divorce it from its readership in the life-giving tradition of the church. I will grant you Bible plus church as the ground for some minimal but necessary infallible authority. But a lonely Bible machine pumping out answers? Never.

Parallel two: The Bible only, *in its literal sense,* is infallible.

With Geneva, as with Rome, make one error and you invite a second. Gussy up the sign, and the first thing you know, you start turning the Mystery into a plausibility. Rome went from an unreal, overblown view of the nature of a church to a forgetfulness of the church's real business.

Geneva goes from a book that never was on land or sea to a Word who communicates in simplicities instead of paradoxes and absurdities, and who, accordingly, within his infallible writings, gives you a world which began in 4004 B.C. and a rabbit who chews the cud.

Really! Is leaving the Mystery business to go into natural history any improvement over leaving it for morals?

17
DELIVERING

LEST IT BE THOUGHT, HOWEVER, THAT THE ravages of transactionalism are confined to the upper echelons of christianity, I want to bring us down a bit to matters which affect more than popes and councils. All this backing away from mystery and filling in with hoked-up signs has as bad an effect on the Indians as it does on the chiefs: In the end, we forget the breath-takingly paradoxical nature of the church. She is—always, everywhere and at once—utterly the Mystery itself, and merely the sign that she is. Unless both are done full justice, we reduce her to a plausibility and make her look ridiculous.

In the literal sense of the word. The church becomes a laughing matter—but laughed *at,* not with. The only fit response a sane person can make to a church which turns her Mystery into a simplicity, and her sacraments into sacred transactions, is ridicule. Explain the act of creation, for example, as an act of starting up, or the act of redemption as a transaction in which the death of Jesus literally buys off an angry God, and you give yourself so many problems that you can be blown out of the water with one well-aimed sneer. Or alternatively, insist that the earthly details of the church's life—her services, her ministry, her day-to-day operations—have some *proper* efficacy, that they are,

135

as what they are, blessings, things of beauty, and unquali-
fied joyfers, and you turn the church into a laughingstock
by the obvious preposterousness of the claim.

But besides turning the church into a bad joke, the twin
mistakes make the church's members hungry and sad. Hungry, because abandoning Mystery deprives them of their
only real nourishment; and sad, because nobody likes to
be laughed at, especially when the ridicule is aimed at overweening claims for merely earthly signs. More than that,
the drift into transactionalism destroys their sense of balance and proportion. Having defined the church's work as
the communication of heavenly transactions through their
delivery of earthly transactions, they corrupt their definition
of what constitutes success for the church. They become
falsely elated over the pieces of business that prosper, and
needlessly depressed over the ones that fail.

All because they assume that the transactions have some
proper efficacy, and therefore will perform like gangbusters,
if only they can get them right. For example: The sign of
the church is people. So far, so good. However, on the
assumption that the sign works in its own right, the temptation is overwhelming to define a successful church as one
full of successful people, and then to proceed to work
especially hard at catering to nice, moneyed, influential
people. I don't care how saintly, how meticulously anti-
transactional, how deeply grounded in the Mystery, any
Christian is: At the roots of his thinking, the success syn-
drome has trained him to prefer a full church to an empty
one, a big church to a small one, a rich church to a poor
one, and a church with clout to one without.

Not that any of those successes is something to be
ashamed of. Let us leave no room here for a cult of unsuc-
cess, for people who think there is something fine about

being lonely, poor and down at the heels. That's just one more missing of the point. The sign is itself, and ought to be done justice. The church should have the best buildings it can afford, the finest music it can manage, the zingiest ministers it can find, and all the money it can rake in. Just because, if you're going to have such things, you ought to develop an intolerance for second-rate performances. But not because the best is any more effective a sign of the Mystery.

I have been, for years, conducting a one-man crusade against mean Muscatel and New York State Port as altar wines. As long as the parish can afford it and the priest has his taste buds about him, we are going to celebrate the Holy Mysteries with a good medium-range Port, imported from the only place on earth so far that produces what my upbringing taught me to call Port. But I don't kid myself for a minute that it makes any difference in the efficacy of the Mystery. In a pinch, I am even prepared, at the price of a tautology and a sprained palate, to use the end of a bottle of Cold Duck. (Lucius Beebe, *ora pro nobis;* Crosby Gaige, *absolve me.*)

But having propitiated these lesser deities in our personal pantheons, we need to return again and again to Mystery as the governing consideration. We have so far referred to it as the building of the City by the Word. But the Bible uses another equally pregnant image: It speaks of the destiny of creation in terms of the Kingdom of God; it teaches us to pray unceasingly "Thy kingdom come." The inveterate temptation of the church, however, is to turn the kingdom, too, into a plausibility—to assume that the church and the kingdom are the same thing, when, in fact, the best that can be said is that the church is the sacrament of the kingdom.

When yielded to, that temptation produces a veritable cornucopia of follies and iniquities. For example: Let us say for the sake of argument that the church may safely be equated with the kingdom and vice versa. On that basis, we may go on to say that, since the unbaptized are clearly out of the church, they are equally plainly out of the kingdom of God. Is that true or false?

It is false, false, very false. The kingdom has been coming from Adam onward. Furthermore, since the King has been here all along, in complete, if paradoxical, charge of his realm, the kingdom has been here too. In the high Mystery of the kingdom, therefore, all men are somehow both in and out of it. Even the unbaptized are in, because it's always been operating; and even the baptized are out, because it hasn't come yet. How much foolishness might we have avoided if we had kept that in mind? How much needless and arrogant bookkeeping? How many wicked prejudices? How many Jewish deaths?

Equating the visible church with the kingdom was a high church folly. Try a low church one instead: The true, invisible church (contradiction in terms there, but let it pass) is the kingdom of God; it is made up of all those who have accepted Jesus as their personal Lord and Savior.

This substitutes a handful of internal, human transactions (prayer, thought, decision) for an external, sacramental one (baptism). It is not, however, one whit less transactional. The Mystery of the Word does not come into anybody's life at a certain time, as the result of a specific invitation. The King does not wait to be asked into his rightful realm. He is there all along. The most you can say is that, on occasion, he sacramentalizes his presence so that the benefits of recognizing it can be enjoyed by his people. How much revivalistic charlatanism might we have been delivered from if we had remembered that? How much spiritual pride? How many boring, saved people? How many foolish campaigns in the church to ram the style of a few down the throats of the many in the name of evangelism?

But that is not the end of the matter. These follies tumble out only to be followed by iniquities. Equating the kingdom with the church, for example, was one of the sleepers in the much-praised nineteenth-century missionary movement. In the back of their minds, many quite admirable Christians conceived of their mission, not only as a bringing of the church, the Gospel and the sacraments to the heathen, but also as a bringing to the heathen of their first contact with the kingdom.

It is instructive to reread the classic nineteenth-cenury mission hymns. I note in myself and others a deep reluctance to use them anymore. Every now and then, somebody tries to give us a bad conscience about that, and says that they bother us because we've lost our missionary zeal. But I don't think that's the reason. I think it's because we have, in the light of history, caught on to the rather arrogant transactionalism that vitiated an otherwise noble movement.

Can we whose souls are lighted
With wisdom from on high,
Can we to men benighted
The lamp of life deny?   (1819)

Fling out the banner! sin-sick souls
That sink and perish in the strife,
Shall touch in faith its radiant hem,
And spring immortal into life.   (1848)

What can we do to work God's work,
to prosper and increase
The brotherhood of all mankind,
the reign of the Prince of peace?
What can we do to hasten the time,
the time that shall surely be,
When the earth shall be filled with the glory of God
as the waters cover the sea? (1894)

Not that you can't put a skin of non-transactional inter-pretation on such poetry: Some of the hymns actually state the Mystery quite well. It's just that you can't sing that stuff for a hundred years and not have it affect your thinking. It's hard to avoid giving yourself the impression that the kingdom isn't going to get to the heathen until you deliver it. Worse yet, it's doubly hard, once you start down that line of thought, to avoid the ultimate language of delivery: war and conquest. We'll do more than just hand it to them; we'll sock it to 'em. Singing good, solid, four-four marching tunes as we go:

Each breeze that sweeps the ocean
Brings tidings from afar
Of nations in commotion,
Prepared for Sion's war. (1832)

And from there, it's only a step to being sure you'll win —to a conviction that by your agency (under God, of course, but by your agency) your now rather strongly eccle-siastical definition of the goal will be achieved.

Then the end! Thy Church completed,
All Thy chosen gathered in,
With their King in glory seated,
Satan bound, and banished sin;
Gone forever parting, weeping,
Hunger, sorrow, death, and pain;
Lo! her watch Thy Church is keeping;
Come, Lord Jesus, come to reign! (1867)

Which means that the kingdom will finally come when the church has finished her temporal conquest, and that it will be marked, as every successful campaign is, by the total rout of all enemies:

Let every idol perish,
To moles and bats be thrown,
And every prayer be offered,
To God in Christ alone. (1859)

It is victory in our time, at our hands. No heathen temple left standing, no church left but The Church, not one Jew, Turk or Infidel left unconverted and *no arguing about it either:*

Let war be learned no longer,
Let strife and tumult cease,
All earth his blessed kingdom,
The Lord and Prince of peace. (1859)

The Mystery of the Kingdom has been scratched and replaced by Christian Chauvinism, out of Ninteenth-Century Evolutionary Inevitability, Ecclesiastical Triumphalism up. But since that bloodline never did have any staying power in the stretch, it quickly petered out. The race was won by Manifest Destiny, out of Pax Britannica, White Man's Burden up. Which, in turn, set us up for the two German wars, and most of what we have had to accept in the name of the only century currently available.

For none of that triumph-of-the-Gospel business was ever about to come off, anyway. Even Scripture seems to say that the kingdom will come, not out of the victory of the church, but out of the shipwreck of the world; that in the end, it is not the church which the Lamb marries, but the whole of creation: the holy City, New Jerusalem, coming down from God out of heaven, prepared as a bride adorned for her husband.

That, of course, is no excuse for welshing on the mission of the church. These earthly sacramentalizings of the Mystery must indeed be held up before every creature we can find. The transport and display of them is a perfectly feasible piece of business, and as with all such transactions, if it's worth doing, it's worth doing well. But it does excuse us from having to believe that the church (however defined, by Catholic or by Protestant) is either the sole instrument or the total extent of the kingdom of God. And that's not only a relief. It's a chance to start rethinking mission. But not here. I owe you an apology.

I am sorry if I have shot any of your sacred cows. I realize that it is considered bad form to take pot shots at such things as the Missionary Enterprise, Evangelism and the Great Commission to baptize all nations. But after all, I do have this new anti-transactional gunsight—and you were the one who painted those silly transactional targets on your cows. Anyway, theologians don't use live ammunition; those were tranquilizer darts. While the cows are

still out cold, get the paint off them. Believe me, they'll look
better without it, and they'll be much less likely to get shot.

For our transactionalism has cost us all dearly. Having
faked the sign of the church and pretended it was something better than it ever could be sticks and stones have
broken our bones and we have been called all kinds of
names. People get angry at us when they find that the
church is full of priests who are flaky, or stupid, or loutish,
or mean, and that the pews are full of half-returned prodi-
gals whose ideas about what constitutes good manners were
formed mostly while they were slopping the hogs.

And we ourselves get depressed when we find that our
cult of the successful church, our trust in the proper efficacy
of our efforts, is just another batch of hogwash. We worry
when people leave the church, we fret when they don't
come in, only because we forget that the church's business
has a *mysterious,* not a *direct,* connection with her life. People come and go for all sorts of plausible reasons. Some
quit because they hate the priest; others join up in order to
hate the priest. Some stay on in the hope of having their
questions answered; others buzz off because they don't like
the answers they get.

And we wear ourselves out trying to control the situation, trying to mollify this one, slug it out with that one,
join forces with fellow partisans, or throw our favorite
rascals out. And it's all fair game. And frequently lots of
fun. And we might as well make a bang-up job of it while
we're at it. But it mustn't be made to matter too much because, after all, it's only matter. It's our business, but its
not our life. We can do it so badly that we end up in the
poorhouse. But we still rest secure in the possession of the
Mystery that never fails.

So no faking of the signs, if you please, and no simplifying of the Mystery. No Chinese restaurant church where you eat plausibilities and feel hungry an hour later. Just the true church—the old leaky bucket, full of the water of life, from which we drink and never thirst again.

18
DUMPING

I FIND THAT I HAVE, MORE OR LESS PARDON-
ably, slipped into usage which, while it is not necessarily
wrong, can be dangerous if it is not recognized as slightly
loose talk. In the interest of brevity, I have frequently said
things like, "In Christianity, religious acts are not transactions in their own right." Properly speaking, however, I
should have been more cautious. For if we are going to
allow my contention that theology is a serious word game,
a groping for the Mystery with verbal tools, statements like
the one just cited should always be modified to read
". . . religious acts *should not be viewed,* or *not be spoken
of,* as transactions in their own right." The point is that
neither I nor you know anything directly about what the
Mystery is, or about what religious acts actually do. We are
simply trying to find the most convenient—or, perhaps even
more modestly, the least inconvenient, the least damaging
—way of talking to ourselves and others about it.

Accordingly, with you thus forewarned that I expect to
be given credit for that subtlety at all times, and myself
thus forearmed against accusations of dogmatism, I return
to my more relaxed usage and take up the subject of the
sacraments properly so called. I propose to elaborate the
following proposition: The sacraments of the church are

not transactions, except insofar as the merely material outward sign is concerned.

Let us clear the board of one matter first. Every sacrament inevitably involves a whole string of transactions—of bits of business which set out to do something and, by proper efficacy, accomplish it. The godmother is a properly effective agent for handing the baby to the priest (though, in all honesty, most women who are not trained nurses can't do it deftly). The altar boy is properly effective for conveying the wine cruet to the altar (though, infuriatingly, he leaves the stopper in more often than not). The priest's ear is properly effective for hearing the words of the penitent's confession (unless he's switched off his hearing aid). And so on. In all the materialities of the sacraments, we are on the plain, everyday, transactional level, dealing in the ordinary, earthly way with things like personnel, inventory, schedules and logistics. There is nothing divine about them. While they may be fancier and more solemn tasks, they involve, qualitatively, no more problems than the work of getting the spaghetti wound around the fork: A proper investment in labor and materials gets the job done every time. You may—indeed, you should and you must—be as transactional as possible. On this level, any other course is fakery.

But on the level of the total effect of the sacrament as Sacrament—when you come to talk about the *benefit* of the sacrament, when you turn your attention from the mere outward sign to the mysterious *inward grace*—there, I contend, you must not be transactional at all. In spite of all the history of transactional talk about the sacraments, and in spite of the almost overwhelming temptation everyone experiences to go right along with it, thinking of them as sacred transactions is bad news. And getting them out of that category is a breath of fresh air. Let me illustrate first with the Sacrament of Penance.

If any sacrament has ever looked, felt and acted like a transaction, it is the bit of business involved in making one's confession to a priest. There you kneel, with a conscience full of sins—with three trash cans labeled Thought, Word and Deed, full of the garbage you allowed to accumulate since your last visit to the holy disposal pit. For a fee (the bother of going, the embarrassment of confessing, and the doing of your penance) the custodian of the dump knocks out your trash cans, puts in new, snow-white liners and sends you out with the advice to live a neater life.

The exercise is transactional in the extreme—and on two fronts. On the one hand, a long-standing tradition held that the confessional was the only dump where you could get rid of really messy garbage, so you had to go there in order not to be caught dead with a rat-infested house. But you were also taught that it had another purpose: Even if you were basically neat, so neat that your trash cans never contained much more than lightly soiled Kleenex and neatly rinsed-out tomato cans, you were urged to go in order that by constantly practicing the act of emptying them, you would eventually become so fastidious that you just wouldn't make garbage anymore. Your trash cans would turn into planters, and you would grow geraniums in them.

Now in fairness, I must admit that the church's doctrine on the Sacrament of Penance has never been put quite as baldly as that. But in all fairness, you are bound to admit that at many times and places, that is precisely the impression which got about on the subject: It was a strange cross between an insurance policy and a self-improvement course. Above all else, it was a piece of business.

But seeing it that way made all sorts of trouble. Protestants accused Catholics of emptying their trash cans just so they could get back to the fun of loading them up again. Catholics accused Protestants of hiding their garbage in their closets. Protestants replied that they got rid of their garbage every night, not just once a month or once a year —and to the Great Dumpmaster Himself, not to some underling. But secretly, both sides had to wonder whether they had done the transaction right. The Protestant, whether he had really repented; the Catholic, whether he had let it all hang out; and both, whether the act they did was sufficient. That is, they assumed that it took some properly efficacious spiritual transaction to get forgiveness. And they wondered, each according to his own lights, whether they had done it up brown. And even if they decided in their own favor, they still both felt the burden of cleanliness: The religious life consisted of feeling good until you felt bad. Which was always pretty soon. None of us takes long to cast the first cat-food can into the nice, clean liner.

It is a fascinating illustration of religious controversy— of how people can be so totally opposed to what they perceive as each other's errors and, at the same time, so utterly united in a third error neither of them sees at all. And it is an instructive lesson in how to resolve religious controversies: Never take them at face value; if people could have made peace on that basis, they would have done so long ago. Instead, look for some unexamined, uncontroverted error in the back of both opposing minds, and attack it. Nine times out of ten, if you demolish that, you cut the foundation from under the original argument, and it collapses of its own weight. My contention here, and throughout the subject of sacramental theology, is that it is unrecognized transactionalism which lies at the base of our troubles. Watch what happens to the Sacrament of Penance when you get rid of it.

The first step is to render the transactional view of forgiveness suspect.

Item one. The parable of the Prodigal Son. As with so many parables, the popular name, because of our penchant for transactions, is exactly wrong. It gets the teaching of the parable a precise one hundred eighty degrees out of whack. This parable is not about the prodigal, but about the father; just as the parable of the Laborers in the Vineyard is not about the laborers, but about the owner of the vineyard. The prodigal is not forgiven as a result of anything he did. Of course, he thinks that's the way it works—and so he composes a terrific confession, full of self-deprecating malarkey about not being worthy to be his father's son anymore, and he hits the sawdust trail home.

"But when he was yet a great way off, his father saw him, and had compassion, and ran, and fell on his neck, and kissed him." He doesn't earn forgiveness by a transaction called Coming Home And Saying You're Sorry. He just walks in and finds he had it all along. The father doesn't forgive him because he made his confession, privately or publicly. He forgives him just because he's his father.

And when the elder brother—another dyed-in-the-wool transactionalist—shows up with his bookful of self-righteous green stamps and complains his father never gave him any premiums, the father, with a touch of impatience, explains he doesn't accept trading stamps: "Look. He's my son; you're my son. Neither of you has to earn any of this stuff; you both already own everything I've got. So what the hell are you standing out here complaining for? Wipe that look off your face and go on in and fix yourself a drink!"

Item two. The Nicene Creed: I acknowledge one baptism for the forgiveness of sins. What does that mean? Does it mean simply that baptism forgives all the sins you've committed up to the moment the water hits you? In that case, it's a bit hard on the kiddies. All the subsequent sins which a baptized infant commits during his entire life will have to be dragged, one by one, before some ticket window or other and processed. If that's the case, it would be smarter to borrow a page from that hard-headed businessman, the emperor Constantine, and postpone baptism until just before death: One blanket policy covers all.

Or could it mean, perhaps, that in baptism we are clothed with a lifelong, head-to-toe suit of forgiveness? Maybe baptism is not a transaction by which forgiveness is given in return for repentance, but rather a sacramental proclamation of the fact that we're always forgiven, always welcome home, and that we will never have to do anything to earn forgiveness. We just have to shut up and accept it. That sounds more like the parable of the Forgiving Father. Perhaps that's what we're supposed to mean when we acknowledge one baptism for the forgiveness of sins.

Item three. In spite of her rather flagrant transactionalism, the church has always hedged a bit on a purely transactional view of Penance. When pressed, she usually admitted that if you couldn't get to the confessional, a sincere repentance would get you absolution anyway. That always looked like an inconsistent concession to the protestant point of view, but it's at least possible that it sprang from an insight into the connection between baptism and forgiveness. Maybe somebody took the view that every Christian walked in a perpetual cloud of absolution, and that all he ever needed do in order to enjoy it was just breathe in.

And there's the word which leads to the second and last

step: enjoyment. Once you get rid of the transactional em-
phasis, Penance takes on a new meaning. It's not a special
piece of business by which you purchase something you
couldn't get elsewhere, but a special kind of party at which
you celebrate what you have always had, but were lately,
perhaps, guilty of neglecting. There are the two of you in
the funny little box—priest and penitent, a couple of perpetually forgiven sinners—telling each other, from different
points of view, incredible old stories about what a friend
you have in Jesus.

Look how many problems that solves. It makes Penance a
real sacrament again—a signal instance of something that
is true everywhere but effectively manifested here. You no
longer have to be afraid of taking too high a view of priestly
absolution. Take as high a view as you like; because when
you do, you will be saying that what is true in the confessional is just as true, and just as effective, clear across the
board. Group confessions, solitary confessions, all confessions everywhere, have exactly the same solemn high access
to the Mystery of forgiveness as auricular confessions.

"Ah, but," the fool says in his heart, "why go to a priest
then, if you can get it anywhere?"

Dummy! Why go to a party, when you can drink by
yourself? Why kiss your wife, when you both know you love
her? Why tell great jokes to old friends who've heard them
before? Why take your daughter to lunch on her birthday,
when you're going to have supper together anyway? Do you
see? What the fool is really asking is, "Why be human, when
you can be a jerk instead?"

The sacraments are there to sacramentalize. Because man
is a sacramental creature and the world is a sacramental
world. The Mystery is everywhere, present in every bit of
business, sacred or secular. But you can't see it, taste it,

touch it, smell it or hear it. And therefore you can't know it. So just to make sure you don't forget it, God takes some agreed bits of business and tells you to make a very careful point of saying that the fullness of the Mystery is effectively present in them. Which of course it is, because it is effectively present in all transactions. And he does that on the sound principle that, for the likes of us, nothing gets done unless we do something about it. The Mystery may be able to hold us without using his hands, but we can't hold him without using ours. And since our relationship with him is apparently supposed to be a two-way street, we need sacraments to keep up our end of the bargain.

I chose Penance for the first illustration, because of all the sacraments, it's the one that has always seemed to make the most overweening claim. But note how that impression got about—and how it is now clean gone. It got there not, as people used to think, because too high a claim was made for confession to a priest: "Some nerve!" they would say. "Where do they get off, having the Mystery of forgiveness funneled through a mere man!" Rather it got there because of the incorrect, transactional rider which Christians too often attached to their perfectly correct, high doctrine of penance: They said, "The Mystery of forgiveness is effectively present in the Sacrament of Penance, unlike anywhere else." Simply change that last phrase to "just as it is everywhere," and four hundred, ever-hating, red-eyed years of sacramental controversy go whistling down the wind.

Why, it almost spoils the fun of being a theologian!

19
ZAPPING

NEVERTHELESS, ON WE MUST—EVEN IF IT costs us our paranoia.

The Eucharist is even better served than Penance by refusing to see it as a sacred transaction. It never did make much sense on that basis anyway. Take, for example, the old assertion that Jesus *becomes* present in the bread and wine. Presto! One more catholic-protestant donnybrook, off to a roaring start. Protestants, made squeamish by what they perceive to be catholic hocus-pocus, insist that Jesus never becomes present in the elements, only in the people who receive them. Catholics retaliate by digging in their heels and going themselves one better: Not only do they say he becomes present; they take St. Thomas's useful substance/accident distinction, turn it into a polemical device it was never meant to be, and go on to claim they even know how he does the trick.

But how foolish! The sleeper in that discussion is the big, fat, transactional word *becomes*. What they both should have said was what Jesus said: This *is* my body; this *is* my blood. Really, Truly, Absolutely. No ifs, ands or buts. Be as high church as you like about it. Affirm his real presence. But don't start throwing around a word like *becomes*. Because that implies that his presence occurs after a previous

153

absence. Keep it up long enough, and you will get a theology in which Jesus *shows up* at mass. And if you're silly, you will get a "spot consecration" theory in which he shows up right between the "r" and the "p" in *corpus: Hoc est enim cor*—ZAP!—*pus meum.* And if you can manage to sucker some equally silly adversary into an argument, he will oblige you by proving that Jesus does not show up between the "r" and the "p," but in the heart of the true believer. Which gives the world two more flawless, perfectly matched, king-size wedges of baloney.

For in fact, there is no sense in which Jesus can be said to show up at communion. Not in a natural sense, for the Mystery of the Word of which Jesus is the supreme sacrament was in the bread, and on the altar, and in the pews, and out in the parking lot, and down in the cesspool twenty minutes before the mass started and ten seconds after the world began. And not in a religious sense, because Jesus, in his Godhead and in his Manhood—crucified, risen, ascended and coming again—is fully present in all the baptized. He doesn't show up in a room from which he was absent. He sacramentalizes himself in a room in which he is already present. The bread and wine of communion are not a peephole through which the church checks out some mysterious stranger who wants to come in for a visit. They are a mirror which the church holds up before her face to see the Mystery which is already inside and at home.

And likewise there is no sense, secular or sacred, in which Jesus can be said to show up in the heart of anybody, believer or unbeliever, true or false. And once you've gotten that straight, isn't it lovely to find the right reason for going to communion again? You don't go because the tankful of Jesus you got last Sunday has now been used up and you need a refill. You go to do precisely what the church has always been smart enough—or lucky enough, or guided enough—to call it all along: You go to *celebrate* the Holy Mysteries. It's the image of the *party* again. You go to taste and see how gracious the inveterately hospitable Lord is. To share still another bottle of the great old wine he's always kept your cellar full of. And to relish once again the old tall tale about how he came to his own party in disguise and served the devil a rubber duck. You go, in short, to have a ball—to keep company while you roll over your tongue the delectable things which have been yours all along, but which get better every time you taste them.

The several sacraments of the church, therefore, are the same party thrown in various circumstances. Call them the Mystery under the guise of a progressive dinner, with cocktails at the Baptisms', soup at the Penances', main course at the Eucharists', and dessert, perhaps with an orgy thrown in, at the Holy Matrimonys'. Or call them Christianity's oldest and longest uninterrupted floating crap game: always the same crowd, the church—militant, expectant and triumphant; and always the same High Roller, the Paschal Mystery, betting everything on one throw and winning. Figure them any way you like. Just don't make them into a bunch of slot machines.

Notice next, however, how avoiding transactional imagery improves your understanding of those less easily defined sacraments which are, in effect, states of life: Holy Order and Matrimony.

If you conceive of a sacrament as a sacred piece of business in which something is cooked up, you quickly become preoccupied with the process by which it is confected. And you just as quickly get drawn off the true center of its sacramentality. The "spot consecration" theory of the eucharistic presence is an example of the distraction, but I want to call your attention to the "moment of Ordination" and the "moment of Marriage" theories, which do even more mischief in their respective bailiwicks.

As soon as you begin thinking of ordination to the priesthood, for example, as a transaction by which priesthood is somehow conferred on the ordinand, you are in for trouble. You begin to convince yourself that a Christian becomes a priest at a certain moment in his life—that priests are "confected" like so many batches of fudge. That done, you proceed to judge whether the priesthood is being exercised in a given church on the basis of the "validity" of the confecting process. And that, in turn, leads you to say that ministers who are not ordained by bishops are not priests. And when all is said and done, that means you are accusing the local Presbyterian minister of peddling bogus sacraments. Which is no way to win friends and influence ecumenical movements.

So take it from the top again and get the transactionalism out. Priesthood is not something you "add" to a Christian. By the baptismal presence of the Mystery of Christ in him, he already has the fullness of Christ's priesthood. The church is a whole kingdom of priests. Notice the benefits so far. We have revived one of the best insights of the Reformation, the Priesthood Of All Believers, an insight on which Protestants muffed the ball because they ended up using it merely as a polemical shillelagh: "The Church of Rome can't turn anybody into a priest; every Christian is a priest already. Just to teach them a lesson, we won't have a sacramental priesthood at all"—forgetting that what's everybody's business is nobody's business, and that an unsacramentalized Mystery simply disappears. So the very people who rediscovered the universal priestliness of the church became the ones who lost all track of the notion of priesthood. This way, how-

ever, we get it back. Furthermore, we get, as an incidental
bonus, the answer to the question "Are women fit subjects
to receive the priesthood?" It is: "Your question is a little
late. They've already got it."

But there are more benefits. Once you free yourself from
the imagery of turning people into priests, you are liberated
from the necessity of taking the ordination ceremony as the
sign of the Sacrament of Order. You stop "confecting"
priests, and you go back to older, better figures. Your priests
are "ordained," "ordered"—that is, they are lined up into
a sacramental *arrangement* within the church. The ceremony at which a person is admitted to that arrangement is
indeed important—once again, simply because you can't do
anything without doing something. But the focus of your
attention now lies, not on the confecting power of the ceremony, but on the sacramental visibility of the arrangement.

Accordingly, the *sign* of Holy Order is taken to be, not
the moment of the laying of the bishop's hands on the head
of a single ordinand, but the ongoing acts of the entire
crowd of those who are in the order of priests. The sign of
Order is precisely the Order itself. The principal normal
manifestation of it is not services of ordination, or letters of
consecration which many Christians never see, but priests
doing the ordinary priesting which all Christians always see.
And that's a better view. It forces us to pay attention to
what's actually happening, rather than fussing about some
quasi-legal entity left over from the past. It might even force
us to think about using priests *as an order*—as a fellowship,
in continuing mutual support—rather than sending them
out one by one, as we do now, in the fond hope that the
tankful of holy gas we gave them in ordination will take
them all the way.

Another benefit is the one which accrues to our thinking

about the ecumenical movement when a non-transactional view of the priesthood is taken. "Moment of Ordination" theories have mired us for years in the problem of figuring out how to arrange a suitable service for the eventual unification of now separated ministries. The problem, to put it bluntly, was how to get some presumably valid bishops' hands on the heads of presumably invalid Presbyterian clergymen—a matter of finding a device for slipping the priesthood over on people who either didn't know they didn't have it or didn't want it at all. Suggestions ranged from having the benighted Presbyterians kneel humbly and gratefully before the True Successors Of The Apostles to having everybody silently lay hands on everybody else and let the Holy Spirit sort it out.

But that's all unnecessary now. If the Presbyterians are already fully possessed of the priesthood of Christ by virtue of their baptismal possession of the Mystery of Christ, and if the sign of Order is the Order of Priests acting as such, then when they act as if they're priests, they'll have valid orders. In other words, all you have to do is concede the ecclesial reality of the Presbyterian Church (they've got no less of Christ than anybody else)—and the rest follows. Best of all, it puts the discussion of the ecumenical movement back where it belongs: It must be a grappling with the nature of the church's life, a wrestling with the question of what kind of sign the church herself is supposed to be. I happen to think that, among other things, it has to be a distinctly priestly sign. But that can't be provided by a service; it can be manifested only by a lot of priesting. As I see it, the job of Anglicans, in the pursuit of church union, is not to give Protestants the priesthood, but to encourage them to exercise it. For my money, when they do that, the job is done—without any mergers, and with no new bureaucracy.

Refreshing, isn't it? Especially if the prospect of a Superchurch gives you the willies.

Lastly, however, Holy Matrimony. Watch how getting rid of "confection" theories gets Mother Church out of the hot kitchen she's been enslaved in for ages.

Perhaps nowhere has the concentration on the "moment of doing the sacrament" done more damage than in marriage. We began by swallowing uncritically the apparently harmless statement that every marriage is contracted on a certain day, at a certain hour. But that was a piece of bait with a very large hook in it. See where it dragged us. The legal imagery of contract led us to see marriage as an extrinsic third something, binding two parties together—when in fact a marriage is simply what two parties do to each other for as long as they do it. That, in turn, tugged at us until we endowed the marriage with a life of its own, and with rights over the parties which the parties could never abrogate—when in fact people with enough nerve have always abrogated any marriage they felt like abrogating. And that hauled us right up onto the beach of never-never land, where we pretended that two divorced people who lived a thousand miles apart, who never spoke to each other, and who were each married to somebody else were still, in the most important sense of the word, really married to each other. And that finally left us gasping the ultimate idiocy: namely, that a man who sleeps with no one but his second wife for the rest of his life is actually a rip-roaring adulterer guilty of mortal sin by definition, and therefore ineligible for absolution.

And this time, our transactionalism got us into more

than mischief. It got us into wickedness. Because this time, we were dealing with people's lives. Not with bread and wine, which you can't hurt, or with the priesthood, where you mess up only a few people, but with warm bodies by the millions, whom you foul up royally if you teach them to pick up the biggest single arrangement in their lives by the wrong handle. The figure of a binding contract is deadly. The most important thing about a marriage is not its confection by a few words and a roll in the hay on some Saturday in June, but the mutual life it brings into being for all the days thereafter. The sign of Matrimony, therefore, should be figured by some image such as Show Still On The Road, or Continuing Partnership, or Ongoing Business Venture: As long as the shop is open, you've got a marriage; when they close it down, you haven't. The business doesn't continue in some shadow existence. It doesn't go anywhere. It just ain't.

And the former partners don't have to ask anybody's permission to get remarried, because in fact they are free to get just plain married—having no present, continuing marriage to stand in their way. When the ongoing sign of a sacrament is gone, the sacrament itself is gone. If a host burns up, you don't have to wonder where Jesus went: The sign is gone, and the Mystery fends for itself until it finds another one. If the mutual life of a couple disappears, you don't have to do any more bookkeeping on the subject of their matrimonial sacramentalization of the Mystery. If they want to go out and provide the Mystery with a new sign, the church's job should be, not to keep sending them bills on the old one, but to help them set up a better shop the second time around.

But look what we did instead. We taught them to see the wedding, not the marriage, as the sign of matrimony. We

told them that at that solemn moment, something vast beyond imagining was confected, probably in heaven. And
then we blithely kissed them off. Out they went, thinking
they were secure because marriage was going to take care
of them—only to wake up, ten or twenty years down the
road, confused and terrified by the discovery that there was
no marriage at all because they didn't take care of *it*. But
they had been well taught: All appearances to the contrary,
they went on pretending they had a marriage just because
they'd had a wedding. And so the marriage that did no job
at all of being a marriage became a prison that every year
did a better job of being a prison.

And there they sat. Angry at themselves for having landed
in the clink. Angry at us for helping to put them there. And
above all, utterly distracted from the one thing they should
have been thinking about all along: how to live their own
lives, on their own two feet, with their own two hands. The
final product of the church's disastrous captivity to the
language of contract on the subject of Matrimony was an
army of emotional cripples, trained from childhood to think
that something which would never exist unless they themselves created it would step out of nowhere and run their
lives for them.

If nothing else ever does, that should teach us how essential it is for the church to mind her tongue.

20
FIREWORKS

AND THERE I COME TO REST. THE THEME OF
this whole book has been precisely the necessity of minding
the christian tongue when we talk about the Mystery. I urge
it upon you.

I do not mean to suggest, however, that you become
finicky to the point of being unwilling to use the old language I have criticized. I myself am perfectly happy to use
any and all of it—to speak of the atonement as a transaction, of baptism as an instrument, of marriage as a contract,
of the elements as converted by consecration, or of deacons
as made priests by the laying on of hands—and I am even
willing, on some days, to say it is all done with a loud Zap!
right on the dot of an *i*. For there is a large grain of truth in
such phrases: They protect us from concocting for ourselves
a religion in which nothing ever really happens. Which
would be manifestly false; for while the Mystery itself is not
a transaction, there is an important sense in which it is nevertheless the supreme happening at the root of everything.

I mean only to suggest that every word—and, particularly, every image—used in theology be examined with the
greatest care and handled with as much judiciousness as we
can manage. The language of theology is a pack of fox-
hounds, and the theologian is the master of the hunt. His job

163

is to feed, water and exercise his dogs so that they will be in peak condition for the hunting of the Divine Fox—and to keep them, if possible, from biting defenseless Christians. He ought to be constantly intent on improving the breed—ready to pay heavily for a promising new bitch, or willing to spend all the time necessary to nurse an ailing but proved one back to health. Above all, he must love dogs—he must be a man who delights in his kennelful of words. For language is the very substance of his profession: If anything can be called the key to the Scriptures, it is a loving study of the images by which all those miles of words are woven into the Word of God.

Someone once accused me of ending every book I have written in the same way and on the same note. I plead guilty. It is the best ending, and it is the ending of the best book. I shall, therefore, use it again: the endlessly refreshing image of Jerusalem, the City of God.

When I spoke, in chapter eight, of the various covenants, their signs and their promises, I promised you a fireworks display at the end. Sit back, put up your feet on the porch rail, and watch.

I have four rockets. I am going to fire them off all at once from the four corners of the lawn, make them come together at the zenith, and then explode them in a single giant shower of sparks. Rocket number one is the sign of the Old Testament: the Ark of the Covenant. Rocket number two is the promise of the Old Covenant: the Promised Land. Rocket number three is the sign of the New Covenant: the Humanity of Jesus. Rocket number four is the promise of the New Covenant: the New Jerusalem, the City of God. All set? Fire!

The *Ark of the Covenant* begins its flight as an image by rising and expanding into a larger image. It becomes the

Tabernacle, the Tent of Witness in the wilderness. But it rises higher still, and when the Israelites actually settle in Jerusalem, it become the Temple. What began as a threatening, aweful box of laws, becomes a lovely, graceful thing, the object of a centuries-long romance: "O how amiable are thy dwellings, thou Lord of hosts! My soul hath a desire and longing to enter into the courts of the Lord; my heart and my flesh rejoice in the living God."

The *Promised Land* takes off as nothing more than a promise in Abraham, but it becomes, in the wilderness, a beauty foreseen: the Land Flowing With Milk And Honey. Moses glimpses it from afar and dies; but the People cross the Jordan and enter it in fact. When they are established in Jerusalem, however, what began as a flirtation turns, year by year, into a love affair. The literal city itself becomes the Daughter of Zion, the beloved of Yahweh, the longing of Israel. Her hills, her gates, even the pools of rain in her streets, ravish the heart: "The Lord loveth the gates of Zion more than all the dwellings of Jacob. Glorious things are spoken of thee, O city of God. . . . the singers also and trumpeters shall make answer: All my fresh springs are in thee." And when the captivity comes, the love only grows greater in the loss: "By the waters of Babylon we sat down and wept, when we remembered thee, O Sion. If I forget thee, O Jerusalem, let my right hand forget her cunning. If I do not remember thee, let my tongue cleave to the roof of my mouth; yea, if I prefer not Jerusalem above my chief joy."

The *Humanity of Jesus* starts as an unimpressive figure in the back of a barn and rises unobserved for thirty years. But gradually it becomes transfigured, multifaceted: He calls his body the Temple and promises to raise it up in three days. He calls it the Bread of Life and feeds it broken to his disciples on the night before his death. He calls it the Brazen Serpent and lifts it up on the cross. And then he raises it from the dead and ascends as the Great High Priest. But strangely, his body does not leave: He makes the church his Body Mystical and, in her, moves across the face of the earth.

The *New Jerusalem,* the heavenly City, makes the most splendid take-off of all: It comes gloriously out of heaven, turreted, pinnacled and gorgeous:

> *Thy walls are made of precious stones,*
> *Thy bulwarks diamonds square;*
> *Thy gates are of right orient pearl,*
> *Exceeding rich and rare.*

But then it rises shimmeringly into the image of the beloved: The City becomes the Bride adorned for her husband and comes in fine linen to the marriage supper of the Lamb.

And with that, all four rockets converge and explode. The Signs and the Promises detonate each other, and the freight of imagery, accumulated over a thousand years, bursts out in one blinding flash: For the Temple has become Jerusalem, and Jerusalem has become the Bride, and the Bride has become the Mystical Body, and the Lamb and his Wife are one. And everything is Christ, and everything is the Bride, and everything is the City where there is no temple, sun or moon, but only the Lamb who is its light. And the River flows back from the dawn of creation, and the Tree of Life returns from Eden, and the Gates of Jerusalem are not shut at all by day, and there is no night there. The tears, the sorrow, the crying and the pain are gone. It is all gardens, gallant walks and silver sounds:

There they live in such delight,
Such pleasure and such play,
As that to them a thousand years
Doth seem as yesterday.

By the drawing of the Mystery, the world has passed from its lostness and found him whom her soul loves. The Beloved comes leaping upon the mountains, skipping upon the hills. The time of the singing perpetually begins.

"Vulnerasti cor meum, soror mea, sponsa; vulnerasti cor meum in uno crine colli tui. Si oblitus fuero tui, Jerusalem, oblivioni detur dextera mea. Adhaereat lingua mea faucibus meis si non proposuero Jerusalem in principio laetitiae meae."

Oh, Wow!